THE SALMON BOOK

THE
SALMON BOOK

DOUGLAS SUTHERLAND

Foreword by
LORD HOME

COLLINS

St James's Place, London sw1

1982

William Collins Sons and Co Ltd
London · Glasgow · Sydney · Auckland
Toronto · Johannesburg

Designed and produced by Breslich & Foss
43 Museum Street, London WC1A 1LY

House Editor and Picture Researcher: Nicholas Robinson
Designer: S A Kitzinger

Sutherland, Douglas, 1919–
The Salmon book.
1. Salmon fishing
I. Title
799.1′755   SH684
ISBN 0 00 216664 X

Filmset and printed by
BAS Printers Limited
Over Wallop, Hampshire

CONTENTS

ACKNOWLEDGEMENTS

I am not normally over generous in making acknowledgements for assistance I have received in preparing a book for publication. In this case however I cannot neglect to express my gratitude to Nick Robinson whose endeavours have gone far beyond the bounds of duty both as editor and presenter.

I am also grateful to Will Garfit, R.B.A. for providing the decorative border on the front of the jacket and the attractive chapter headings.

Douglas Sutherland, Scotland, 1982

LIST OF ILLUSTRATIONS

The author and publishers would like to thank the private individuals, photographers and picture libraries who have provided illustrations. Special thanks are due to Jenny Macarthur and Denis Tilley at the *Field*, Major Brian Booth at the Tryon Gallery, and Major E. R. W. Robinson. All other sources are credited in brackets below.

FOREWORD

Douglas Sutherland has fished in many of the freshwater rivers of the world, and from all the sorts of fish gives pride of place to the Atlantic Salmon. Few will quarrel with his choice, for it gives incomparable sport to the fisherman, and is undeniably good food.

But he fears for the survival of the species, and with reason, for the modern poacher is not like his ancestor who 'took one for the pot'—nor is the netter like his predecessor who operated in the river estuary, and therefore had an interest in conserving stock. Now the former is armed with poison and explosives, and the latter with nets of invisible nylon fibre which in the sea can stretch for 1,000 yards or more.

Mr. Sutherland's account of the natural casualties as *Salmo Salar* migrates from the spawning shingles of the Scottish rivers to their feeding grounds in the waters off Greenland shows very clearly the damage to stocks which will result unless commercial exploitation of the salmon is curtailed. It can be done, but it will need a firm will and some legislation.

As to the art of angling the author, being an experienced practitioner, prefers experience to theory. If the local ghillie advises a Jock Scott for a dull day, and a Silver Doctor when there is a glint of sun, then the visitor will be wise to conform until he has learned his own lessons.

He is content too to let the philosophy (or madness) of those who practise the skills come out of the mouths of poachers and lairds and ghillies, men, women and amateurs in many an entertaining anecdote.

And what does it all add up to? Patience—yes. Keeping the fly in the water—certainly. The frustrations which in retrospect are as satisfying as the triumphs—true. For the tales which linger and satisfy are of those monsters which 'got away'.

But all in all Douglas Sutherland is content to find the secret in St. Peter's 'I go a-fishing' and that is in truth enough.

Home, 1982

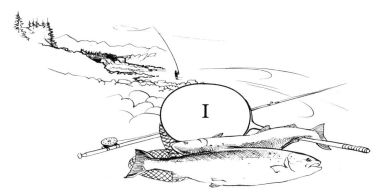

THE FISHING GAME

*'Salmon fishing is a game which a man and a fish must play together.
And while a man can dictate the terms on which the sport shall be enjoyed
he sometimes forgets that the fish has the absolute power of veto.'*

Richard Waddington, 1959

There is an almost irresistible temptation for a dedicated salmon fisherman like myself to start a book like this with an extravagant flourish. 'The salmon', one might write, 'is The King of Freshwater Fish, the *ne plus ultra*, incomparable in its majesty, supreme, unchallenged, the original Triton amongst the minnows, the gamest of the game.'

It would not be true, or true only to the most blindly dedicated of *aficionados*.

Who would deny that the sudden scream of the reel, the first wild rush and the heart-stopping explosion of silver, glistening in the moonlight as a big sea trout takes the lure is not amongst the greatest of thrills, sending the blood pounding in the head and setting the adrenalin flowing.

Who would claim that to stand for fruitless hours up to the waist in freezing water with icicled hands and leaden feet, compares in enjoyment with a gentle day in June when the brown trout are rising and the soft clouds drift idly against a blue sky, when God is in his heaven and all is well with the world.

Yet, of all the great tribe of salmonidae, *Salmo Salar*, the Atlantic Salmon, is for me the most fascinating.

Although our North Atlantic Salmon has never ventured up any of the rivers which empty into the Mediterranean, Pliny the Elder (A.D. 23–79) knew him as *Salmo Fluviatilis*, the salmon of the rivers and he described him as 'the River Salmon the most preferred of all sea fish by the inhabitants of Aquitaine.' For centuries after Pliny, the salmon ran up the Garonne in Aquitaine in great numbers. Alas, no more.

Three hundred years later, Ausonius, when a prefect of Gaul, knew and evidently appreciated the salmon of the Moselle River.

> Nec te puniceo rutilantem viscere, Salmo
> Transierim, latæ cujus vaga verbera caudæ
> Gurgite de medio summas referuntur in undas
> Occultus placido cum proditur æ quote pulsus.
> Tu loricato squamosus pextore, frontem
> Lubricus, et dubiæ facturus fercula cœnæ
> Tempora longarum fers incorrupta morarum,
> Præ signis maculis capitis, cui prodiga nutat
> Alvus, opimatoque fluens abdomine venter.

I hope Latin scholars will forgive this less than perfect attempt at translation!

Nor will I pass thee over, Salmon, thou of the pink-red flesh whose broad tail carries you upstream to the head waters and whose lashing betrays your presence under the calm surface. Thou, of the armoured scales and slippery body can provide a most delectable course of an excellent meal and keep fresh for a long time. You of the distinctive spotted head whose great paunch trembles with overflowing fat.

Pollution down the years has banished the salmon from all but a few of the once sparkling rivers of France, and, indeed, almost all Europe. Not only do salmon no longer run up Ausonius's Moselle or the Garonne, but they are extinct or almost extinct in Denmark, the Netherlands, Portugal, Switzerland and Germany. In France and Spain, the runs are only a fraction of what they once were. In the United States, the total catch from natural runs of Atlantic salmon in 1976 was just over 1000 fish. This in a country where prolific rivers such as the Connecticut and Merrimack held salmon in quantities that rivalled the major European rivers. Above all, that cosmopolitan river the Rhine is an example of destruction on a massive scale. Now totally polluted by industrial waste and rendered impassable by dams and weirs, it was once the pride of Europe. As Anthony Netboy has recorded in his *The Salmon*, as late as 1885 the nets in the area of Kralingen in Holland took a total of 69,500 salmon averaging 17.1 pounds. In the light of this, it is interesting to read an account by a great English Inspector of Fisheries, Frank Buckland (who had a museum of 'Economic Fish Culture' in South Kensington and was an industrious recorder of exceptional fish) of a netting station on the Rhine.

Mr D. van Elst, who lives at Rotterdam, holds a lease from the government of the fisheries on the Maas, the only one of the three mouths of the Rhine through which Salmon migrate. The principal fishing station is at Orange Nassau, about fourteen miles from the sea; the river is here about nine hundred yards in width, and the nets used eight hundred yards long, thirty feet in depth, and the meshes two and a half inches from knot to knot, or nearly ten inches in circumference. This gigantic net is worked by a steamer of twelve horse power and a windlass driven by two horses on shore; the fish are not at once killed, but

13

Contrasts in salmon fishing: (*above*) the Lune in spate crowded with
local fishermen and (*facing page*) the Carrots beat on the featureless
Wye below Hereford.

are kept alive in a well-boat, which is towed to Kralingen, three
miles from Rotterdam, and there sold alive to the merchants.
There are five private fishing stations above Rotterdam: three
are worked by steamers and horses. The nets are only worked
during the ebb tide.

Buckland goes on to say that the Rhine fish were in excellent

condition and often weighed forty, fifty and even sixty pounds.

Closer to home, the sad story of the Thames indicates what pollution has done in banishing the Salmon from many of its old haunts. The few records that exist show that in the middle of the eighteenth century the salmon runs still provided a respectable living for the netsmen. In one day in the summer of 1749 more than 30 fish were caught below Richmond Bridge and as late as 1798 there were more than 400 professional fishermen working on the river.

At the turn of the century, however, the river went into a rapid

15

decline, as the diary of the man who held the fishing rights at Boulter's Landing at Maidenhead shows. Between 1794 and 1821 he caught 7,346 lb of salmon, but against a catch of 72 fish in 1804 and 60 fish in 1806, he recorded only 2 fish in 1821 after which his diary falls silent. The last salmon was caught in the Thames some time in the late 1820s or 1830s and, according to Buckland was bought by George IV for a guinea a pound.

Today, most of the English rivers emptying into the North Sea are salmonless. Before the Industrial Revolution, the Tyne surpassed the Tweed in excellence. Now only the West Country rivers, notably the Wye, can hold a candle to the waters of Ireland and Scotland.

Happily, the story is not one of unremitting gloom. Scotland, Norway and Iceland still possess rivers which the salmon run up in almost the same quantities as they have done for centuries. A number of polluted and dammed rivers have been cleaned up and re-opened. Although there is no doubt that the future of the salmon is in jeopardy for a number of reasons which are explained towards the end of the book, there are grounds for feeling optimistic. One thing is beyond question. The sportsmen who fish for salmon with rod and line and the netsmen who make an often precarious living in the estuaries are the greatest potential force for conservation.

Just when salmon fishing started to develop into a sport in these islands, as opposed to being primarily a method of acquiring food, is hard to identify. Even the origin of the word Angle is obscure to a point which renders conjecture profitless. It has even been suggested, without much conviction, that it derives from the method of fishing used by the early Angles. Personally, I have always disliked the word, feeling, irrationally, that it suggests some sort of deceit—particularly irrational, of course, as all fishing entails attempting to deceive the fish.

Certainly by the seventeenth century, angling for fish of all sorts had become established as a country sport and the earliest books on how to master the art started to appear.

Thomas Barker in *The Art of Angling* (1657) gives advice on making artificial flies to catch salmon. Dame Juliana Berners, the formidable prioress of St. Albans, had also mentioned the use of flies as lures in her famous *Treatyse of Fishing with an angle* (1496), but rather as an afterthought. She principally recommended worms and 'a sovereign bait that breedeth on a waterdock', whatever that may have been.

Barker records catching a salmon on the Thames with the aid of his new-fangled 'winch' and also using a landing hook, which is the first recorded mention of what we know today as a gaff.

Barker's winch must have been some sort of primitive reel. Up to that time the fisherman attached his lure to the end of his rod by means of a length of horsehair plaited up to fifteen times or more. One can only think that either the fisherman of those days were more skilful than their modern counterparts or the salmon a deal more naive.

Richard Franck and Robert Venables, both soldiers in Cromwell's Army, were enthusiastic experimenters in different patterns of salmon fly and their tours of duty, both in Ireland and Scotland, must have given them an unusual opportunity for those days of testing their efficiency in such widely contrasting rivers as the broad Shannon and the majestic Tay.

Although it was only in comparatively modern times that a more efficient substitute for horsehair became available, there is no doubt that equipment became steadily more sophisticated from the mid-seventeenth century onwards and experimentation with different types of lure ever more varied.

Izaak Walton, a contemporary of Franck and Venables, was

probably the greatest experimentor of all. Like a medieval alchemist he burnt the midnight oil in devising many and wonderful pastes and potions in the hope of finding the piscatorial equivalent of the Philosopher's Stone. There is little evidence that he fished for the salmon, which he described as the King of Fish, by any method which would be deemed legal today, but his ingenuity cannot but command reluctant respect.

Few people perhaps know the full title of Walton's great classic. It is: *The Compleat Angler or the Contemplative Man's Recreation. Being a Discourse of Fish and Fishing, Not unworthy the persual of most Anglers. Simon Peter said, 'I go a fishing:' and they said, 'We also will go with thee.' John 21.3.*

Perhaps, as a title, on the long side to be commercial nowadays, but it seems to me to say it all. Or, then again, perhaps not quite for John 21.3 continues 'They went forth, and entered into a ship immediately; and that night they caught nothing.'

That certainly says it all!

To me Walton has little appeal in his long technical discourses on the merits of this or that method of catching every freshwater fish that swims. 'Angling' he wrote, 'may be said to be so like mathematics that it can never be fully learnt.' The day that I spend my leisure by the waterside endeavouring to solve mathematical problems will be the day that I sheathe my rod forever.

Old Izaak did not have it all his own way, even before the day of the anti-blood sports brigade, if for different reasons.

Dr Johnson, who regarded the greatest felicity in life to be a chair in a congenial club, declared angling to be a matter of 'a stick and a string, with a worm at one end and a fool at the other.'

Lord Byron, who was more at home keeping company in a warm bed, described angling as 'the cursedest, coldest and the stupidest of sports.' He went even further, describing Izaak as a 'sentimental savage', continuing:

18

A salmon fisherman tackles a falls pool in the late eighteenth century.

And angling too, that solitaire vice
Whatever Izaak Walton sings or says:
The quaint old cruel coxcomb, in his gullet
Should have a hook and a small trout to pull it.

Today there are more sentimental savages who prefer to spend Saturday afternoon by the waterside with a fishing rod in their hands than turn out on the terraces to watch that other national bloodsport, football.

19

Far from being a 'solitary vice' fishing is the most sociable of sports. It is also one of the most competitive. Those dedicated souls whose life is match fishing and who sit for hour after hour on their alloted pitch striving to achieve the heaviest catch, even if only by a matter of ounces, are no more or less competitive than the Rolls Royce set who migrate annually to the exclusive salmon beats and spend the rest of the year boasting of their triumphs or bemoaning their failures. They are all brothers of the angle under the skin.

Even at this distance of time, my competitive spirit gains a little satisfaction that even the great Walton and his boon companion and arch rival Charles Cotton did not always return home triumphant:

> The river Dove flows down its Dale,
> And ripples just as sweetly,
> As when good Master Walton hied,
> With Master Cotton by his side,
> To angle there compleatly.
> And sometimes Master Walton scored,
> And sometimes Master Cotton;
> But sometimes neither caught a fish,
> When Walton sadly murmured 'Pish!'
> And Cotton muttered 'Rotten!'
>
> (E V Lucas)

Though Walton described it as the Kind of Fish there is little evidence that he fished for salmon, at least by any method that would be deemed legal today. In fact, it was only two centuries later, with the onset of Queen Victoria's reign that the dedicated salmon fisherman emerged as a recognisable 'species' in his own right.

A man who matches the great Izaak in charm, eccentricity and expertise is the author of *Days and Nights of Salmon Fishing in the Tweed* (1843), William Scrope (pronounced Scroop). Although he fished on the Tweed for twenty years or more and wrote the first classic work on deer-stalking, Scrope was far from being the amiable old buffer that he appears. As a young man he studied painting in Rome and like many men of his time was able to discourse on a variety of subjects at once. The page headings of his book on salmon fishing give some indication of this: 'An Innocent Mistake', 'Koran of Mahomet', 'Tranquillity', 'Landscape Painting', 'Claude and Salvator Rosa', 'The Cauld Pool', 'Poussin', 'Pure Genius', 'A Voracious Salmon', 'Monstrum Horrendum'. Scrope was also an old friend of Walter Scott's and used to set off with the celebrated author's 'faithful right-hand man', Tom Purdie, to 'burn the waters' of the Tweed in the middle of the night, doubtless after discussing the merits of *Ivanhoe* over the port.

By the end of Scrope's life interminable wrangles were beginning to break out about the merits of different techniques. Scrope did not care much how he caught his fish though he seems to have preferred the fly to all other lures. With the emergence of the idea of a right and a wrong way to catch salmon, it may be said that the sport came of age.

The right way to catch salmon was, indisputably with a fly. The high priest of Victorian salmon fishing was the immensely bearded and moustached George Kelson, who always fished in a bowler hat waterproofed with two coats of size and Acme black. Kelson, incidentally, is not only remembered as a great salmon fisherman and as the author of a magnum opus on the salmon fly, but as the man who, in 1863, hit the first century for Kent since 1847! He and his contemporaries used massive greenheart rods which, fully kitted out with reel and line, must have weighed 3, 4 or even 5 pounds,

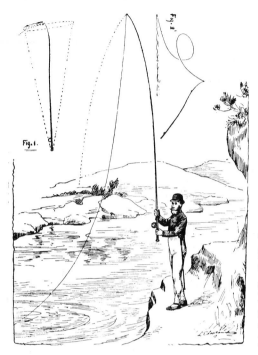

The futility of instructive book illustrations demonstrated by George Kelson, in this case the secret formula for the Switch Cast. Rather endearingly, the line-drawings in his books showing the 'correct method' are all portraits of Kelson himself.

and were capable of prodigious feats. On the River Ness, a certain Alexander Grant cast 65 yards without shooting any line with a 21-foot rod which he had specially designed on the principle of 'vibration frequencies of violins', no less. This design was famous as the 'Grant Vibration Rod' and in case the reference to violins sounds improbable and frivolous, it is worth pointing out that Grant corresponded with Albert Einstein on the subject of mathematics.

Grant also invented a method of fishing with a floating line called the 'oiled-line' technique at around the turn of the century. At the same time, another great fisherman of the day, Percy Laming, was experimenting with smaller rods (down to 14-foot) and lighter lines fishing near the surface with which he swung the fly around in front of the salmon's nose. This method he christened 'controlled drag' and very successful it was too. Fishing on the Aberdeenshire Dee between 1897 and 1923 for about a month each year he caught 2,203 salmon—giving an average of three fish a day, though he probably fished with a sunk fly for some of the time.

The acknowledged 'father' of modern salmon fishing with a floating line was A. H. E. Wood who had the Cairnton beat on the

The pioneer of greased-line salmon fishing, A. H. E. Wood, looking both opulent and confident on his beat at Cairnton on the Aberdeenshire Dee.

Dee for a great many years and devoted himself to the delightful occupations of salmon fishing and being a millionaire. Wood pioneered what he christened the 'greased line' technique after observing salmon rising to white moths in Ireland in 1903. He was not, as is often thought, the first to stumble on the fact that in summer conditions salmon will move further to the fly and are more susceptible to a smaller pattern than they are in the spring. Laming was using a floating line in 1897 and Alexander Grant developed his oiled line before that. But Wood's method has gone down in history because he was insatiably curious. He refined the greased-line method over a number of years, fishing on the same stretch of water and noting when it worked, how it worked and why it worked. His fame is also, in all probability, partly due to the fact that he was extremely hospitable, and though it is said that he reserved the best pool at Cairnton for his exclusive use, he invited many great fishermen to stay such as Ernest Crosfield and J. A. Hutton as well as numerous friends and acquaintances.

The period from about 1880 to 1930 was the great age of salmon fishing. The devoted sportsmen of the era are a worthy subject of a book in their own right. They caught such prodigious quantities of fish that it is difficult to imagine anyone ever repeating their feats—even if the salmon still ran up the rivers in the same numbers. George McCorquodale of Dalchroy caught 8,924 salmon on the Spey alone between 1891 and 1935, and his grand total must have been well over 10,000. Robert Pashley who lived on the Wye caught 9,800 salmon on that river between 1906 and 1951. All the fishermen I have mentioned often caught upwards of 400 salmon in a year. It is the sort of achievement that requires time, money and persistence. It also requires an extraordinary degree of skill. Salmon fishing, the trout fisherman often claims, is a matter of luck. If the water is the right height and there are fish in the river, then it is simply a matter of dangling a monstrous concoction of brightly coloured feathers in front of the salmon's nose. Nothing could be further from the truth. Although *anyone* can catch a few salmon in ideal conditions, it takes a very great expert to catch salmon throughout the season—in the depths of February when the rod rings are icing up and the big 'springers' are lying deep and reacting slowly, or in the droughts of July and August when only the grilse can be tempted with a slimly dressed Size 10 Blue Charm from the edge of the rapids.

The great fishermen caught salmon consistently. The ordinary, holiday fisherman will be delighted to land three or four fish on a good day when the river is settling down after a spate and a new run has entered the river. When the spate runs away to nothing he will curse his luck with the weather and expect to catch very little. The great names, and many of their contemporaries knew how to capitalise on taking fish, and how to winkle out stale ones in impossible conditions. Of course, when they were in the right place at the right time, the results could be extraordinary. Ernest Crosfield, who, besides fishing for salmon throughout the British Isles was a fine shot, stalker and big game hunter, spent 20 days in the summer of 1902 fishing on the Ellidaa River outside Reykjavik in Iceland. During his stay he caught 299 fish, but it is not so much the grand total as the individual day's catches which make interesting reading. They run as follows: 2, 5, 2, 18, 2, 3, 4, 21, 16, 20, 5, 15, 40, 23, 17, 5, 24, 4, 4, 5. When the fish were taking, he 'took' fish. And where lesser mortals might have inscribed words like 'bonanza', 'corking day' or 'suicidal fish' in their fishing diaries, on the day he caught 40 Crosfield merely wrote: 'Calm, dark and drizzle, fished No. 3 (beat), caught 17 from top rat hole to saucepan and 18 in skyline; 13 of these after dinner without moving 20 yards.'

But for me, salmon fishing is not a matter of accumulating huge 'bags' and fishing every single day of the season. In particular, as I totter in old age, the competitiveness becomes less and less important. For that reason I have no intention of describing many of the great salmon fishermen who are still alive today. Some of them you will encounter later in this book, such as Richard Waddington, whose thoughtful books on salmon fishing are mentioned in the chapter on salmon flies, Charles Ritz, John Ashley Cooper who has fished so extensively in Iceland and elsewhere, and of course, Lord Home who has provided the elegant foreword. If you want advice of the most practical kind that will help you to catch salmon, then you should read the practical books on the subject, or better still, watch some old hand on the river bank. This is a book about the salmon and about the sport of salmon fishing, not *how* to catch them.

The salmon is the most magical fish of all and the whole atmosphere of salmon fishing holds an irresistible attraction. Not only the still imperfectly understood mysteries of the salmon's life cycle, but the big fish caught or lost, the eccentricities of ghillies, the wiles of the poacher, the adventures in far-off waters and the ever-changing moods of familiar rivers exert a fascination which anyone who has ever joined battle with Salar the Salmon will understand.

And if you are truly in search of advice, then remember the wise counsel of William Scrope, for the sake of the salmon and for the sake of your fishing:

Keep *Close time* strictly; kill no spawning fish; tamper not with the foul ones of any sort; preserve the fry; send the black fishers to Iceland [black fishers being poachers with 'blacked up' faces, though why Scrope should wish them on the fishing

26

'Just in the dubious point where with the pool/Is mixed the trembling stream . . ./There throw, nice judging, the delusive fly.' A fisherman takes the advice of the eighteenth-century poet, James Thomson. Even streams as small as this can provide exciting sport in a spate.

paradise of Iceland I do not know]; but catch as many salmon as you can, *recte si possis* (meaning with a rod), *si non quocunque modo*—that is, with a net or leister, and so forth.

Rather like an old-fashioned salmon fly, this is as sound now as it was in Scrope's day, though most of us would omit the second Latin tag today.

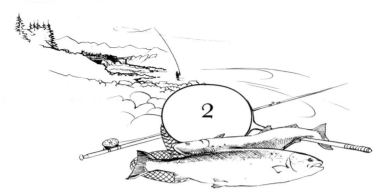

THE LIFE CYCLE OF THE SALMON

*'Nature directs them to salt waters, as Physick to purge and cleanse them
. . . from all their muddy terrene Particles and Gross Humours, acquired
by their extraordinary excessive Feeding all the Summer in fresh Rivers.'*
Robert Hewlett, 1706

For a fish which has graced the tables of epicures down the centuries and has for so long been regarded as the ultimate prize by the game fisherman it is surprising how little has been known of the habits of the salmon.

That our more remote ancestors should remain incurious about its life cycle is perhaps understandable in the days when it was only regarded as a welcome addition to the larder and its method of capture a matter of indifference.

With the development of salmon fishing as a sport, however, and the search for ever more attractive offerings to induce the salmon to take, it might have occurred to someone to investigate why the fish took in the first place.

It is true that as long ago as 1706 Robert Hewlett published a book called *The Angler's Sure Guide* in which he paid some attention to the habits of the salmon, from which the following passage is taken.

For salmon being Fish of Prey and Great Feeders, Nature directs them to salt waters, as Physick to purge and cleanse them, not only from their impurities after Spawning, but from all their muddy terrene Particles and Gross Humours, acquired by their extraordinary excessive Feeding all the Summer in fresh Rivers . . . and when they are fatted and glutted with their long excessive Feeding in Fresh Rivers, and have spawned in the latter end of the Year, repair to the Sea for Warmness, and to be purged of the gross Humours by the Calidity of the Saline Water; and when Winter is over, return to their Summer Habitations.

Good stuff one might think, were it not for the fact that far from being 'fatted and glutted with their long excessive Feeding in Fresh Rivers', salmon do not feed in freshwater at all.

It was only towards the beginning of the nineteenth century that it became generally accepted that from the moment the salmon started to run upstream to spawn they ceased to feed and continued their fast until they returned again to salt water the following spring.

This at first sight would seem so improbable that even today there are those who would seek some alternative explanation of why no salmon caught in fresh water has ever been found to have any food in its stomach.

As a boy I was fortunate to have fished on many occasions with the late Archie Grant of Carron. The fact that I was only a young lad armed with a trout rod whilst the grown-ups fished for salmon did nothing to diminish my pride at being allowed on the river bank in such company.

Archie was of the school who found it hard to accept the fact that salmon starved themselves in fresh water. One of the greatest fishermen of his time who would catch salmon when everyone else returned to the fishing hut empty-handed, he was a great believer in having the correct fly or spinner for the state of the water or the mood of the fish.

If, as the general argument goes, a salmon only snaps at a fly out of irritation or playfulness and thereby gets itself hooked, why should it one day snap at anything in sight and next day at nothing at all. Even more telling in Archie Grant's view was the question of why a fish should repeatedly ignore the irritation of having a large gaudy Thunder and Lightning repeatedly dragged past its nose but suddenly take offence at, say, a small Blue Charm.

I remember once standing by, my trout rod abandoned, watching Archie's methodical, perfect casting of a fly upstream on one of the lower stretches of the Dee. The water was gin clear and even I with my implicit faith in my hero was watching to observe his technique rather than in any real hope that he would hook a fish, when he was taken with a bang.

The fish then 'dug in' and, straining upstream against the hook, remained quite motionless so that we could both see him quite clearly. As we watched the fish emitted from its mouth an opaque cloud of fluid before making a dash for the deeper water.

'There you are,' cried Archie triumphantly 'that's food he's digested and is spitting out.'

I was reminded of this incident on re-reading The Revd W. Houghton's classic work *British Fresh-Water Fishes* originally published in 1879 and now happily republished in a splendidly produced single volume. The Revd Houghton would accept nothing as fact that he had not personally proved to his own satisfaction and examined the contents of the stomachs of many hundreds of salmon. Although he found great quantities of sand eels, young herrings, shrimps and other food in the bellies of sea-caught salmon (including on one occasion as many as five large herrings) he confirmed that he had never found any solid food in a salmon in fresh water.

Another authority, W. L. Calderwood, who was Inspector of Salmon Fisheries for Scotland, recalled in 1938 that he had encountered four instances of food in rod-caught salmon since the beginning of the century. They were, respectively, 'a trout in a salmon caught in Loch Shiel, a char in a salmon taken, if I remember rightly, in Loch Tay, a trout in a salmon caught in the Thurso, and five parr taken in a salmon caught in a tributary of the Tweed'. Calderwood also mentioned seeing a salmon that topped the Revd Houghton's five-herring fish by three more. He was, however, crystal clear on the subject of salmon feeding in fresh water: 'If a man meets me only at four funerals in a dozen years, is he to conclude that I make a habit of going to funerals.'

It now must be accepted as certain that the salmon relies on 'its great paunch trembling with overflowing fat' to sustain it on its journey to the spawning beds. And this is not so surprising as it may appear at first. Herrings also have long periods of fasting and male seals on their rookeries at breeding time take no food at all. Of course, none of this helps to explain quite why the salmon should fall prey to the fishermen's lures, but that remains one of the several mysteries which surround this extraordinary fish.

In the migration of the salmon back to their breeding grounds they display an extraordinary tenacity in negotiating any obstacle placed in their path. They are capable of incredible leaps to overcome natural hazards like waterfalls and their ability to do so in the heaviest of water bears witness to their remarkable strength.

The tagging of fish, which is now a widespread practice, has shown that although there are some instances of them running up rivers other than their parent stream, by far the majority return to the gravel beds of their birth. This raises for me an interesting question.

Every year many hundreds of salmon desert the mainstream of the Tay to run up the Braan, a tumbling rocky stream which joins the Tay just by Telford's elegant bridge at Dunkeld. Now this would be natural enough were it not that about a mile up the Braan it cascades over a waterfall of such formidable height as to make it quite impossible for even the strongest of fish to overcome it. Yet year after year they make the attempt. It is an awe-inspiring spectacle to watch them hurl themselves vertically out of the water only to fall back bruised and battered onto the jagged rocks below. It is not unusual to see five or six great fish in the air simultaneously. As it is quite impossible that their breeding grounds should lie above the falls what atavistic instinct impels them to attempt the impossible leap?

I do not know whether they then return to the Tay and resume their journey to its headwaters via the comfortable salmon ladder thoughtfully provided by the Hydro-Electric Board at Pitlochry, but if so it only makes the whole business more difficult to understand.

Just how high a salmon is capable of leaping is a vexed question. Some observers claim to have witnessed jumps of over ten feet, others insist that five feet is nearer the mark. But I do not think it is really possible to have a *puissance* event for salmon. If you watch them leaping a waterfall, they jump clear of the tumbling water, then fall against it and seem to swim vertically. And do not ask why salmon jump in the middle of perfectly flat pools. There are a host of answers which range from the itching of sea lice to fear of one sort or another. On the whole, though, it is rather like asking why birds fly.

After swimming and jumping their way to the headwaters of

The frayed gills and gill maggots of an undoubted kelt.

the river, the salmon select their spawning grounds with care. Their requirements are for light gravel beds in free-flowing water. The gravel stones must be small enough to be easily moved by the female fish to form the hollow 'redd' in which she deposits her eggs and free of any form of sediment which might clog up the flow of the water between the stones. As they are being laid they are fertilised by the male lying alongside. The eggs are then covered over and left to their fate.

The ritual of the laying and the fertilising of the salmon's eggs carried out in shallow water is a dramatic spectacle as the female flings herself broadside to the stream, her silver flanks throwing up a glitter of spray as she writhes in the spasms of birth.

The average number of eggs laid by the female is estimated at around 600 to 700 per pound weight so that for a fish to deposit around 10,000 eggs is not unusual.

From the moment the eggs are laid the salmon become kelts, or more correctly the female becomes a kelt and the male a kipper, although the name kipper is little used nowadays. They then start the long journey back to the sea usually in January, February or March. As they descend the later travellers meet the 'clean' fish running up.

Kelts are, of course, uneatable and when caught must be returned to the water. As they readily take almost anything offered to them they are a cross the fisherman has to bear reluctantly.

Nothing is more galling than to play and land a vigorous fish only to discover that it is a well-mended kelt. Most kelts, however, are poor emaciated creatures which can be reeled into without a struggle. Many of them never reach the sea at all and it is a sad sight indeed to see these once splendid fish putrefying on the shingle banks, prey for carrion crows and black back gulls.

In their attempt to regain the sea the spent Atlantic salmon differ from their Pacific cousins, such as the Sockeye and the Chinook.

These fish, which swarm up the great rivers of Canada and Alaska in vast numbers, are strictly on a one-way ticket. They arrive at their spawning beds, gaunt and emaciated and having spawned die slowly and miserably. In this they resemble the migratory eel which returns to the unknown deeps under the Sargasso Sea after its European sojourn to procreate and die.

The Pacific salmon, incidentally, belongs to a separate genus, the *Oncorhynchus* meaning 'hook-nosed' and does not really have a place in this book. Buckland (the worthy with the museum of 'Economic Fish Culture' in South Kensington) called him

'Californian', which might be regarded as an unwarranted slur in some quarters, and wrote uncharitably: 'As regards the Californian salmon, I do not know yet sufficiently about him, and what I have seen of him I do not like.'

In the case of the Atlantic Salmon the number who eventually return to spawn for a second time is very small indeed. Perhaps as low as 5 per cent, though this figure varies in different rivers.

The hatching of the eggs which the parent fish have left carefully covered over in the redds takes place in early Spring. For a short period of three to four weeks they remain in the gravel feeding off a yolk sac, rather after the fashion of an emerging chick, and are called alevins. When the yolk sac is finished they emerge into the world as fry and rapidly find it is a very cruel place indeed.

Large numbers die from starvation or lack of *lebensraum* and those which survive are harassed by predatory birds and cannibal fish. Perhaps as few as 10 per cent of the eggs laid become fry and fewer still attain the next stage when they become parr. The massive losses amongst fry and parr are frequently due to overcrowding. One of the greatest benefits that can be conferred on any salmon river is the expansion of the spawning grounds, either by dynamiting waterfalls or building fish passes. The spawning grounds of most salmon rivers today are on barren moorland, with insect-harbouring trees only on the lower reaches of the river. The parr require a large area in these shallow stony streams over which they can roam in search of food.

At this stage in their life they are almost indistinguishable from the young of the brown trout. This can sometimes present the fisherman with a dilemma. Trout eat salmon fry and, when they grow larger, parr too. Trout, therefore, should be knocked on the head, taken home and eaten for breakfast. But in the case of young trout the matter is not as straightforward as one might imagine.

Victorian authors went to great lengths to distinguish between the two species. They pointed out that the spots on the trout are 'distributed over the flanks without regard to the medial line', whereas in the parr, there are few if any spots 'on the body below the medial line with the exception of a few immediately behind the gill-covers'. But as these traditional distinctions are tedious, technical and utterly impractical, I will not repeat them all here, save to say that the advice occasionally given, that the scales of a smolt or parr will rub off and those of a trout will not, is probably the most certain way to permanently damage a young fish as could be devised. The accompanying illustration showing the different

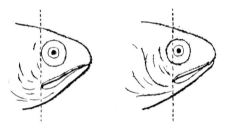

Heads of a young trout (*left*) and a parr (*right*). The maxillary bone extends to the rear edge of the eye or beyond in the young trout, but only a little further than the centre of the eye in the parr.

positions of the eye is probably the surest way of telling a young trout and a parr apart. On the whole, though, it is hard enough to keep the wriggling, leaping and gasping little creatures still to make a reasonable identification. Even then there is no way of telling a young sea trout and a young brown trout apart. The best advice, in fact, for any fisherman who hooks a parr or young brown trout is not to take it out of the water, but to grasp the fly between finger and thumb and shake it loose. If this does not work, *wet your hands*, and try to work the hook out. Then gently place the fish back in the water. There is, I believe, little point in killing the young trout, and while you are debating their identity, a young salmon is probably expiring in your hand.

The parr grow to between about 3 and 4 inches in length and normally spend from two to three years in fresh water, though this depends on the supply of food. In the Icelandic and Canadian rivers, with their short summers and long winters, the parr frequently remain four years in the river. Then, usually in late Spring, they start to take on a distinctive silvery colour and begin their migration down to the sea. At this stage they become known as smolts.

On their passage to the sea the smolts are easy prey not only for fish-eating birds like the merganser, the heron and the cormorant which can eat its own weight in fish in a day, but even greedier predators like the pike. The survivors who reach the sea can only be a tiny proportion of those which started out on their dangerous journey.

Once the smolts enter salt water they set about the business of feeding with a will, first of all mainly on plankton and, as they grow bigger, sand-eels, sprats and other fry.

For some reason that nobody has so far been able to fathom, when the smolts reach estuarine waters they divide into two distinct sections which might be described as the home and away teams.

During the next twelve to fourteen months the home team remain close inshore feeding so greedily that they grow from minnow size to a weight that is normally between 3 and 7 lbs. Then the following Spring they return to the fresh water and are known as grilse. In the opinion of many, pound for pound they are the gamest fighters when hooked and certainly the finest of all for the table.

Meantime, the away team disappear far out into the Atlantic, so far as can be established largely heading for the rich feeding grounds off the south-east coast of Greenland. Some may return after two years at weights between 5 and 20 lb. Others remain to grow to enormous sizes. Although the official British record for a salmon caught on rod and line stands at 64 lb, there are certainly some very much heavier fish, some say up to 100 lb, but that is the stuff of which fishermen's dreams are made.

No one is quite sure what the salmon feed on so greedily. Most authorities on the subject have had their pet theories, from small squid, prawns, capelin (a small fish found in Arctic waters), elvers and herring. It seems most likely, though, that the salmon is aggressively omnivorous and, rather like the marauding Assyrian of old, will descend on any creature smaller than he is with gusto.

Confusingly, it is not possible to tell the home and away teams apart by size alone. Admittedly netsmen and fishmongers distinguish a grilse as anything less than 7 lb and a salmon as anything weighing more. This is entirely arbitrary. Grilse of up to 14 lb have been recorded, and salmon down to 3 lb.

Fortunately, every fish carries with it a detailed autobiography in the form of its scales. Each scale displays the life story of the fish, or at least the index to that story, in the form of rings. These may be read in the same way that the rings of a tree can be read, though the inquisitive fishermen will need a microscope or powerful magnifying glass. The principle of scale reading is simplicity itself.

As the parr grows in size, the scales also grow and form a series of ridges and furrows which appear under the microscope as light and dark rings. As it grows quickly in the summer months the rings become further and further apart, but as autumn merges into winter they begin to contract. The scales of a full-grown salmon, therefore, show, at the centre, the rings of the parr and the smolt. These appear as a dark area with particularly dense bands representing the winter months. After two, three or four such

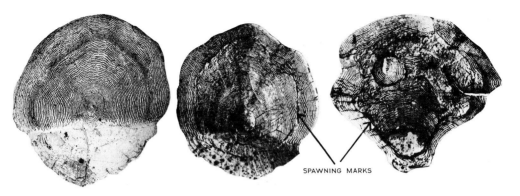

SPAWNING MARKS

Left: the scale of a maiden fish which has spent two winters in the sea. *Centre:* the scale of a previously spawned hen fish, showing the spawning mark. *Right:* the scale of a previously spawned cock fish. A rare sight since the great majority of cock fish die after spawning.

bands, the rings suddenly expand. The next dark band represents the first winter in the sea, the next the second winter and so on. Most salmon spend two or three winters in the sea, with five being about the maximum. On the scales of a grilse, therefore, only one winter at sea is recorded.

It is also possible to distinguish salmon which have spawned previously by scale reading. A broken line called a spawning mark appears quite clearly on the scale and in rare instances there may be two or even three. The oldest recorded Atlantic Salmon ever caught came from Loch Maree on the West coast of Scotland. It was thirteen years old and had spawned four times. This was a very exceptional occurrence indeed.

Lucky, though, is the salmon that attains such an age. Even in the sea the salmon is not free from persecution. Although the smolts rapidly grow to a size when they can no longer be preyed on by fish such as the cod, the seal is a constant enemy, particularly when it returns to the estuaries and tries to negotiate the fixed nets of the salmon fisheries.

There is an increasing lobby against the culling of seal pups. It is certainly a very emotive issue although one is tempted to say based on sentiment rather than science. Nor does it fall within the scope of this book other than to remark that the war of attrition waged against the seal by the net fishermen is not because they begrudge the seal the odd fish but because of the immense damage they do to their nets. A seal trapped in a net in pursuit of a salmon will tear great holes in it whilst escaping which can cost the fisherman dear to the extent of endangering his livelihood.

Much also has been made recently of salmon disease. Of the various diseases to which the salmon is prone certainly the most menacing is UDN (ulcerative dermal necrosis). The most recent outbreak which occurred first in the 1964–65 season in south-west Ireland and rapidly spread to almost all salmon rivers in Scotland was considered to be so serious as possibly to result in the extinction of the species. Certainly the effect on some rivers was devastating, and as in the case of myxomatosis in rabbits, a harrowing sight.

In fact, there is evidence that although UDN has only been scientifically defined in recent times, it has in fact been a recurrent phenomenon over the centuries. It still does not make it any less alarming.

Of the many ills to which the salmon is heir there is now an even greater menace in the activities of the deep sea netters. With their modern equipment they can locate the great shoals of salmon in the deeps and measure their catches in tons rather than pounds, but that is something we will come to later on in this book.

In the meantime we can only marvel, as its enemies multiply, that the salmon continues to survive. Long may it continue to do so despite the gloomy predictions of the prophets of woe.

THE SALMON FLY AND OTHER TACKLE

'*At times Salmon will take anything, at times nothing. In a fever of excitement the King of Fish will exercise his royal jaw upon a thing it were an outrage to call a salmon fly. A one-sided, wobbling, hydrocephalic bunch of incongruous feathers.*'

George Kelson, 1895

There is no length to which the inexperienced salmon fisherman will not go nor any expense that he will spare to improve such equipment and lures as are acknowledged to be legitimate. Controversy rages about the rival merits of various types of reels and lines. With the constant advances in technology, rods appear on the market every few years for which higher and higher degrees of perfection are claimed.

As surely as the twisted horsehair of yesteryear has developed by stages to the finest nylon, so the trusty old greenhearts have given way to the cane, the fibreglass and now the hideously expensive carbon rods.

You can equip yourself with every type of technological wizardry and complicated gadget that the tackle shops will be delighted to sell you. You can wear a jacket that inflates into a life-raft complete with alarm whistle and iron rations, then you can obtain at great expense a reel that winds up the slack line at the touch of a button, that infernal gadget an automatic tailer, magnetic fly boxes, a wading stick with a handle made from antlers and a priest made of extra light alloy but hard as tungsten steel.

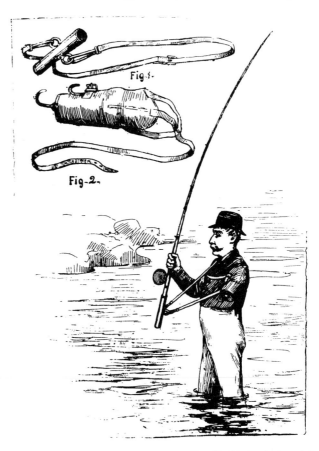

A late nineteenth-century device called The Necklace, designed for 'the use of Anglers who have unfortunately been deprived of one arm'. Fig. 1 shows the socket in which the butt of the rod was placed for long casting or playing a fish. The apparatus in Fig. 2 was attached after a fish had been hooked, which presumably provided an entertaining spectacle for passers-by and an extra chance for the fish.

If you are going to do it properly, you should have no less than three rods (15 ft., 12ft. 6in. and 10 ft. 6 in.), three reels and two lines each for the larger rods (sinking and floating) and a floating line for the 10 ft. 6 in. rod (all of them incidentally double taper).

Essential equipment for the tyro: an amphibious car on the Tay in 1964.

In short, you can make any tackle dealer a very happy man indeed by thinking that you must have just the right equipment to catch salmon. The worst of it is that you should. If you try to fish on the Tweed in the Spring with a 10-ft. rod and a floating line (because it is all you own) then you certainly will not catch as many fish as your opponent on the opposite bank who is casting an effortless 35 yards at every attempt with a 15-ft. carbon fibre rod. On the other hand, if he is weighed down with the inflatable life raft, indispensable oil skins, hook sharpener, thermometer, Swiss Army penknife with the gadget for-taking-stones-out-of-horses'-hooves and so on, then you can reassure yourself that he probably is not having so much fun.

All I can do is describe the equipment I possess. I do not suggest you imitate the list. Like the kit belonging to anyone who has fished for a long time, it is suited to certain rivers and certain conditions; it has, so to speak, evolved. I am fond of it in the same way that one might be fond of an old and faithful spaniel, but that is not to say that if it disappeared overnight I would go out and buy as nearly the same again as possible.

One 15 ft. Grant vibration rod. The Grant rod is spliced together with leather thongs and I inherited it from an uncle. I only once took it to bits and had to take it to Malloch's in Perth to have it put together again. I have never taken it down since.

One built cane 14 ft. fly rod. It has the sort of joints you screw to lock. Much easier to take down than the other sort.

One 12 ft. fly rod. Ditto.

A pair of waist high waders which have a tear in them at thigh level. Always take them with me. Never use them.

A pair of thigh waders with leather hobnailed soles.

A pair of green rubber knee-high boots with little straps which theoretically you can tighten. Personally I've never tried.

A Barbour waterproof jacket with a rather smart if somewhat frayed corduroy collar and press studs.

I also have a *leather belt* with a large metal buckle which says Texas on it. (No, I don't know why.) I clip things onto it like a landing net when trout fishing, a priest which looks more like a policeman's truncheon and an extending gaff.

There is a *tailer* which won't lock onto anything and I usually wear it round my neck at risk of strangulation. I only carry this in

HEAD GEAR.

BURBERRYS,

31, Haymarket, London, and Basingstoke.

"THE FIELD."   "THE SPORTSMAN."

Showing plan of DOUBLE BRIM.

"THE GOLFER."   "THE SQUIRE."   "THE ARUNDEL."

"An exceedingly light fishing hat—as perfect as anything of the kind could be. The double brim answers admirably ; the gut collars are kept secure from the effect of light and damp (their greatest enemies), and always ready for use."—THE FISHING GAZETTE.

Sporting style: Burberrys have always provided excellent hats, but seldom have they provided shelter for such elegant moustaches.

the kelt season as those enormous landing nets carried by boatmen are impractical for the pedestrian.

A *tweed hat* in which I never stick flies except sometimes by mistake.

Then I have a very large *fishing basket-cum-canvas* bag in which I carry two spare reels, one with a white floating line and one ponderous thing with a sinking line and a very loud ratchet which makes a very loud racket indeed on the few occasions I have hooked a fish whilst using it. My other reel, with which I generally fish has a nice purr and I think was made by Illingworth before he went wrong and started making spinning reels.

A circular metal box with fly casts and bits like split shot.

Sundry fly boxes.

A smallish *leather wallet* which has scissors in it and places for other useful tools all long since gone missing.

A very large *whisky flask*.

This list is obviously not exhaustive. It does not for example include a thing my wife gave me for some long-gone Christmas which was designed to facilitate the removal of hooks from fishes mouths and has since quite inexplicably become lost. All I have tried to do is include the essentials.

Also, as the alert reader will have noticed, this list contains no spinning rods, Devon minnows, spoons, Abu multiplying reels, prawn mounts and so on and so forth. I am a fly fisherman not a bait-fisherman. In the same way, I prefer whisky to gin, port to brandy, claret to burgundy and brunettes to blondes. It is a matter of taste.

In the early days in this country, as in most others, by far the greatest number of fish were netted, speared or otherwise dispatched for their value as food, rather than for sport. In terms of centuries, the comparatively recent development of sport for sport's sake has brought with it the sportsman's tradition of giving the quarry a fair chance of winning (or to be more accurate, escaping). The greater the speed that driven grouse can be induced to achieve, the higher a pheasant can be persuaded to fly, the greater the challenge. Every sportsman has a number of personal rules that he adheres to for his own pleasure and satisfaction. I fish for salmon with a fly. This does not mean that everyone else should fish for salmon with a fly, except on those rivers where it is obligatory.

None of the items of tackle mentioned above leads to a greater variety of opinion nor to a greater degree of experimentation and controversy than the contents of the fly box. The bait fisherman with his preferences or prejudices for spoons or artificial minnows or prawns or whatever, can never be in the same dilemma as the fly fisherman who has literally thousands to choose from and who can, if none of the existing patterns satisfy him, sit down and tie his own creation.

Irritatingly the tying of flies is not one of my skills. I have the most beautifully long artistic fingers but for fly tying they are not. My brother who has fingers which resemble nothing more than a bunch of bananas ties them exquisitely.

The date when artifical flies were first used to catch fish in this country can never be established. Certainly it was long before the time of Dame Juliana Berners whose *Treatyse of Fishing with an Angle* published in 1496 is generally quoted as the first recorded writing on the subject.

Claudius Ælianus writing in the fifth century records:

> I have heard of a Macedonian way of catching fish and it is thus: between Beracea and Thessalonika runs a river called the Atraeus and in it there are fish with speckled skins . . . These fish feed on a fly peculiar to the country, which hovers on the river . . . Now, though the fishermen know of this, they do not use these flies at all for bait . . . They fasten red wool around a hook and fix on to the wool two feathers which grow beneath a cock's wattles and are like wax in colour.

And old Claudius was quoting from a source already 400 years old!

In the eighteenth and nineteenth centuries there was a generally held belief that the larger the species, the larger the fly should be. Thus river trout flies were small, sea trout flies larger and salmon flies larger still, sometimes to the point of the ridiculous.

Until the beginning of the nineteenth century most flies were whipped directly onto the line which made changing flies a very tiresome business indeed. Later the cast was attached to a gut eye which still had its disadvantages in that it was perishable and many a good fish must have been lost by the gut eye giving way. It is only in the last eighty years or so, so recently in fact that many gut eyes flies still lurk in some old misers' fly boxes, that the metal-eyed fly as we know it today was introduced.

But these technical improvements were as nothing when compared with the re-thinking on the actual presentation of the fly itself. In the eighteenth century the tier of flies was largely limited by the availability of local materials. The body was most often made of pig's wool and the wing from the feathers of the turkey, the heron, a variety of game birds or wildfowl. The oldest salmon fly in existence is largely made up of peacock tail and pig's wool.

Writers such as Thomas Tod Stoddart, the author of *The Angler's Companion to the Rivers and Lochs of Scotland* (1850), and one of the anonymous contributors to *Jones's Guide to Norway* (1848) give examples of some early patterns. Many of the flies in *Jones's Guide* do not have names. They are simply listed under numbers such as No. 5:

Hook: No. 8.
Tag: Orange mohair.
Body: One half orange pig's wool, the other half brown pig's wool.

Ribbed: Gold twist all the way up.
Legs: Two plain red hackles.
Wing: From the Red-tailed Kite.

Then the heartening comment is added: (N.B.—This is a wonderfully good fly.)

Similarly Stoddart gives patterns under numbers, or under the titles of particular rivers. The Dee fly is composed of:

Body: Blue mohair, dark brown hackle, silver twist. *Wing:* Speckled black and white turkey feather; for small sizes of hook employ teal feather.

Tail or Tufts: Yellow or red. *Observations:* Wingless hooks, like Palmer flies on a large scale, are, I understand, sometimes used on the Dee and Don, by salmon-fishers.

At this time, almost every pattern was tied for a particular river and for a long time were not accepted on any other water. The Aberdeenshire Dee even had its own type of long-shanked hook, which presumably was supposed to hook better in that river's streamy water.

Both *Jones's Guide* and Stoddart's *Angler's Companion*, however, give examples of the 'named' flies, such as The Childers ('So called after Colonel Childers, a celebrated sportsman and frequenter of Tweedside') and The Parson both of which incorporated exotic materials such as blue macaw, black cockatoo, green parrot and bustard.

The names, incidentally, are worth commenting on. Many flies take their names from either the inventor, as in the case of the Akroyd developed by Charles Akroyd of Brora in Sutherland specifically for the Dee, or Jock Scott after a Tweed boatman or, rather after the fashion of rose-growers, in honour of an individual like the Lady Caroline after Lady Caroline Gordon-Lennox, daughter of the Duke of Richmond and Gordon of Gordon Castle on the Spey. One wonders whom that splendid fly mentioned by William Scrope in 1843, 'Meg with the Muckle Mouth' (i.e. Meg of the Big Mouth) was named after.

Scrope gave the pattern for a fly named after the celebrated wizard Michael Scott 'whose fame as a powerful magician had spread over most part of Europe' and who had 'cleft the Eildon hills in three'. It must, as a result, be the only salmon fly that can be found in Dante:

> Quel' altro Michele Scoto fu, chi veramente
> Delle magiche Frodi seppe il Gioco.

The dressing for anyone anxious to try out its magical powers is:

Wings: Mottled feather from the back of a drake.
Head: Yellow wool, with a little hare's fur next to it.
Body: Black wool.
End of the body: Fur from the hare's ear; next to the hare's ear crimson wool.
Tail: Yellow wool.
Round the body: Black-cock's hackle.
End of the body: Red-cock's hackle.
Round the body: Gold twist, spirally.

Throughout the nineteenth century, the patterns of salmon flies became more and more complicated, more colourful and the materials increasingly exotic and obscure. This may have been partly because there was no point in trying to imitate a natural fly when it was realised that salmon did not feed in the river. More likely, though, it was due to the greater numbers of feathers and furs available and the variety of the tiers of flies.

With the publication of George Kelson's vast tome *The Salmon Fly* in 1895, fly-tying emerged as an art, not a craft. It certainly seemed to have little to do with catching fish. At times, Kelson seems to have been writing about painting rather than fly-tying:

... The laws of colour enter to warn us that an equal division
of any two colours in a fly by no means leads to a necessarily
harmonious result. For instance, a smaller portion of blue or of
yellow in opposition to a larger one of yellow or blue, may
establish a harmonious combination more apparent than two
exactly equal portions of these colours. We must decide, in
view of the general effect, what colours shall go side by side,
and how much of each, in proportion to the whole. There is a
harmony of *balance* and a harmony of *contrast*.

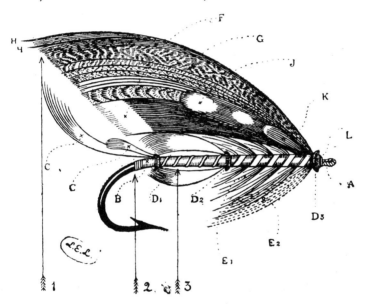

George Kelson's analytical diagram illustrating the parts and
proportions of a salmon fly. The numbered arrows show: 1. the
'proper length of tail and wing beyond the hook-bend'. 2. the 'place
of the first coil of the tag relatively to the hook-barb'. 3. the 'place on
the hook-shank (relatively to the hook-point) at which the ends of the
gut-loop should terminate'. 'No;' wrote Kelson, 'if your fly is not
symmetrical it will not obey you, and if all your tackle does not obey
your brain, art and science are banished from your sport. Away goes
skill—in comes *chance*!'

Working on the principle that '*Order* is nature's first law, and it is certainly that of every good Salmon-angler', Kelson described and classified the salmon fly in six categories according to the different types of wing and provided an analytical diagram illustrating the parts and proportions of the salmon fly.

Kelson and his contemporaries went to extraordinary lengths to obtain just the right materials for their flies, convinced that a spot of red here or a dash of blue there was the infallible recipe for success. 'To my mind', wrote Kelson, 'the best black and white *speckled* hackle is taken from a Rail (*hypotoenidia torquata*), which is a native of the Philippine Islands; and the best black and white *barred* hackle from the Banded Cymnogene (*polyoroides typicus*), found in Africa and Madagascar.'

There is something rather splendid about the way the Victorians, quite ingenuously, treated the Empire as their oyster. Even individual birds are singled out. For example a bustard shot by Mr Mowbray M. Farquhar in Matabeleland early in the season of '95, is praised as 'the best bird I ever saw', and then we find a Mr George Horne of Hereford cross-breeding Amherst and Golden pheasants in order to obtain black dots rather than black bars on the tail feathers. All in the interest of fly-tying. Perhaps this relentless pursuit of the right formula is nearer to alchemy than either art or salmon fishing.

Today, of course, although flies such as the Jock Scott, Green Highlander, Silver Doctor and other classic mixed wing patterns are to be found in most fly boxes, the majority of salmon flies are simple constructions of one or two colours made from dyed bucktail. The swing away from the complicated Victorian dressings came about with the introduction of A. H. E. Wood's greased line technique. Wood used much simpler flies such as the Blue Charm oddly reminiscent of Stoddart's Dee fly, or the March

Brown tied on Low Water hooks. He even experimented with what he called 'Toys' which merely had a few turns of silk round the shank of the hook, a tail of golden pheasant topping and perhaps a turn of ostrich to form a 'butt' over the bend of the hook. But the ultimate refinements were the Redshank and the Blueshank, simply hooks painted respectively red and blue. And he caught fish on them too, though not without some effort.

All the salmon flies mentioned so far are what, for the sake of convenience, may be called 'traditional' patterns. There are several thousand dressings of this sort. They represent nothing in particular, though the salmon probably take them because they resemble one or other variety of small fish, or because their pretensions have an irritation value.

Since the Second World War, treble hooks have become increasingly popular. There were the Waddington flies, introduced by Richard Waddington in his *Fly-Fishing for Salmon* (1951). The principle of the design of these flies is that the treble hooks are linked to the end of the shank and the standard patterns such as the Thunder and Lightning or Silver Wilkinson are simplified and adapted so that the wing is wound round the shank in the form of a hackle, i.e. there is no top or bottom to the fly. Waddington himself recorded great success with the first professionally designed batch on the River Garry in Invernesshire in 1950. Until the end of March of that year, he and his party caught 47 salmon on traditional patterns, lost 96 and pulled a further 34. In April and early May, using the Waddington design, they landed 55 fish, lost 4 through breakages, pulled 3 and lost only 1 through the hooks pulling out. Over the same period the traditional single hooks accounted for 13 fish landed, 27 lost and 1 pulled. Waddington claims that his fly swims more evenly and hooks better than the traditional flies. Wood made the same claim for his Low Water patterns, so did Kelson before him for his perfectly proportioned mixed wing flies.

The Waddington flies have, by and large, been replaced by tube flies and Esmond Drury trebles, almost universally tied with hair wings. Hair wings have become a fashion in the last twenty years or so, and many fishermen today use only three or four different coloured hair wing tube flies tied in a variety of sizes. But they are really no different from the traditional patterns. The Hairy Mary is only a simplification of the Blue Charm and the Stoat's Tail a revised version of the Sweep. There are still many hundreds of different patterns in general use, some more effective than others on bright days or dull days, in peaty water or water so clear that you would happily use it to top up the car battery. To every fisherman his personal favourite.

It often seems that it would be more illuminating to discover why a fisherman uses a certain fly rather than why a salmon takes that fly. A certain fly may work wonders for one fisherman and prove fruitless for another. Very often it will be found that, quite illogically, the fly on which an individual caught his first fish remains his staunch standby for the rest of his fishing life. It all goes back to a question of the confidence of the fisherman rather than the interests of the fish.

Like many other fishermen, I started my life-long love affair with the sport in pursuit of brown trout. The first time I graduated to a 'grown ups' river from our own little burn, my mentor, the kindliest of men, tied a cast for me consisting of a March Brown, a Silver Butcher and, inevitably, a Greenwell's Glory. I caught twelve good trout. Beginner's luck, of course, but to this day I tie exactly the same cast on the first day of the season every year and will continue to do so simply because it gives me confidence, or maybe even more simply because I am superstitious.

FLY-DRESSING

Stout Party—'What do you think of that?'

Swell Friend (prophetically)—'Pooh! nothing but a kelt would look at
such a thing.'

OUR FRIEND TRIES HIS PET FLY

Stout Party—'I have caught a very long salmon!'

Keeper—'That's a ful fish and a kelt; and ye maun be fined five
pounds' (*his jaw drops*).

The choice of fly, then, is almost entirely a matter of confidence. There are many fishermen who chop and change their fly with such frequency that they seem to spend more time with their line out of the water than in whilst they rummage in their tackle boxes in an agony of indecision. Ten minutes with one fly and no sign of action and they start getting fidgety.

On the other hand, there are a few who stick to one fly come hell or high water. This is perhaps carrying loyalty too far, but I know which man I would bet on to catch the most fish.

I like to think that I personally strike a happy medium between the two schools of thought, but perhaps this is more by accident than design. It so happened that a few years back I hung my fishing basket above a paraffin lamp in a Highland bothy where I was staying with the result that the whole thing caught fire and an accumulation of many hundreds of flies which I had in old-fashioned fly books perished in the flames.

It was a sad if spectacular end to many old friends and I must confess that I do not have the same superstitious affection for my present modest collection.

I do not have more than perhaps a couple of dozen different patterns of salmon flies and none of them of obscure or romantic origin. I do however set great store by having each fly in several sizes from very large to very small. Why on certain waters and under certain conditions a salmon will go for a small fly and ignore a large one or vice versa I do not pretend to know, but I am sure size is of much greater importance than colour.

Did I say there was nothing in my fly box which was neither obscure nor romantic? This is not quite so. I have one fly which is dressed largely with the hairs from my old friend the late Sir Compton Mackenzie's beard and nothing could be more romantic or obscure than that.

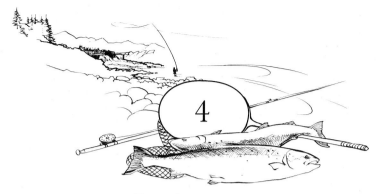

BIG FISH

'It took the three of us to lift it out of the water and it was the ugliest great brute I ever saw. It was quite black on the back and had an immense hook on its jaw . . . the nearest we could make it was 103 lb and 2 oz.'

Anon., c. 1901

Let it be established straight away that the official record for a salmon fairly caught on rod and line in this country is that of Miss Ballantine's cock fish of 64 lb, caught and weighed before witnesses on the 7 October 1922 on the Glendelvine beat of the river Tay.

There will, however, always be considerable doubt about the size of the largest salmon ever taken in British waters, or, for that matter, anywhere else, if only by reason of the whispers about monstrous fish taken at dead of night by the light of a poacher's moon. The unwillingness of any miscreant to own up to the taking of a fabulous fish is understandable, although there are many who might prefer to pay the magistrate's penalty in return for immortality.

The greatest of these nocturnal leviathans, and perhaps the most believable, is a great cock fish taken in a net in the year 1901, or so it is said. The story of its capture was told to W. L. Calderwood, the Chief Inspector of Scottish Salmon Fisheries at the time and one of the most authoritative and reliable writers on salmon. His second-hand account is as follows:

The late Mr Roderick Anderson, of Anderson Brothers, who had a fishing tackle shop in Princes Street, Edinburgh, and who happened also to act as the Hon. Sec. of the Curling Club to which I then belonged, a man from Dunkeld, and who often spoke to me of salmon matters of interest, told me one day that an old soldier who made baskets and fishing creels had caught a monster of a fish. He said that it had been caught illegally, and that the man came into the shop from time to time for orders. I asked him to telephone me the next time the man came, and to let him know that I would like to hear about this fish, also that the information would not be used against him but would be regarded by me as a matter of natural history.

It was three weeks or a month later when I heard that the man was waiting in Anderson's shop, so I went there at once. I found a tall man with a quiet, respectful manner, an evident old soldier, but not one of the wild sort by any means. The first thing to do was to establish friendly relations and confidence, after which the story came out somewhat after this fashion:

'There were three of us fishing the mouth of the Devon with a net, in the month of December, when we caught this fish.' The Devon, I may explain, flows into the tidal estuary of the River Forth some miles below Stirling, and the date of the incident was 1901. 'It took the three of us to lift it out of the water and it was the ugliest great brute I ever saw. It was quite black on the back and had an immense hook on its jaw and a large head. We had nothing to weigh it with, but, of course, we knew that it was a quite exceptional fish, so we took it up to a neighbouring farm and got it weighed on the farmer's scales. We weighed it with great care and the nearest we could make it was 103 lb. and 2 oz.'

When I asked what had been done with the fish, I learned

to my great regret that it had been cut up and distributed, and that no outline or tangible record had been kept.

In the late 1930s, writing to Jock Scott who was compiling a book of game fish records, Calderwood added: 'We do not know anything as to the accuracy of the farmer's weighing machine, but even if it were a pound or so out, the fish would still be a record. On the whole I was inclined to accept the whole story . . . the fish taken by one Willie Walker in a sparling net in the Tay estuary comes next.'

Willie Walker's fish is reputed to have weighed 84 lb, and to have been taken in the winter of 1869 a few miles above the Tay bridge, on the north side of the estuary. No permanent record of it was made, except for some outlines cut out of wood which, according to Calderwood again, decorated the doorways of various salmon bothies till they fell to pieces. He also commented that 'the event was so important in Willie Walker's life that he could talk of little else so long as he lived'.

Whether Willie Walker gazed at his prize fish rapturously until it rotted away to nothing is not known. In all probability it was sent off to market with unseemly haste and kept him in 'strong liquor' for some time to come. Enormous salmon certainly appeared on the market throughout England from time to time, though as often as not their place of origin was ignored, as a delightful letter in the 16th July 1881 issue of the *Field* makes clear:

A MONSTER SALMON

Sir—I am desirous of communicating to you the intelligence of a leviathan salmon having been received by one of the fishmongers here about a fortnight ago, the dimensions and weight of which are so extraordinary, and the evidence of their trustworthiness so unquestionable, that I trust you will consider the subject a fitting one to be recorded in your columns.

This salmon was purchased from the fishmonger by a restaurant keeper in Market-Street, here (an old and most respectable house and worthy landlord). I got the first information about this monster from Mr Ramsbottom, fishing tackle manufacturer here, when I called upon him on Saturday last. He told me he had seen the fish and had spanned it with his hands; but had not seen it weighed. Mr Ramsbottom's description of the fish's length and dimensions and reputed enormous weight interested me very much and determined me to obtain every information I could about it. I have therefore seen both the fishmonger and restaurant keeper who sold and bought the fish, and my examination of them separately have given to me details in regard to it which practically corresponds with each other.

I have seen the entry in the restaurant keeper's day book, which records the receipt and payment for the fish, which is as follows: 'One salmon, 4ft. 6ins, 82 lb 14 oz, £4 15s.' This correspondents with the information given to me by the fishmonger, with the exception that he says the length was 4ft 7½ins, and the girth at shoulders 34in. The fishmonger likewise told me that he had first asked five guineas for the fish which he thought it was worth as a 'show' one (it was exhibited in the restaurant keeper's window, and it was there Mr Ramsbottom saw it); but eventually he sold it at the weight and price mentioned, allowing at the same time the odd 8d. (£4 15s 8d) to which the above weight and price swung out. The transaction was a ready-money one, so that no account passed between seller and purchaser. As to where the fish came from, the fishmonger could tell me no more than that he had got it from Carlisle, and upon my asking whether he could show me an account for it, he told me he never 'bothered' with accounts, as all his transactions, both purchases and sales, were made in ready money. The fishmonger, however, promised to write to his Carlisle correspondent for this information, which I shall be glad to communicate to you hereafter should you think it worth while. From what the fishmonger told me abundant further evidence could be produced as to the weight of the fish. He tells me it was a wonder in the market while there with the other fishmongers and the public, and that many shillings and glasses were won and lost about its weight.

Mr Ramsbottom tells me the fish was a fresh-run one, in good condition, though in no wise remarkable in that respect, and that it was a male fish. Will you kindly say how the above weight, &c., compares with previously well-authenticated monsters salars. What a pity a plaster cast was not got from it.
Manchester, July 17   W.B.

The largest salmon taken in the British Isles of which we have reliable evidence is a fish netted in the Tay estuary in 1870 weighing 70 lb or more. The different accounts of its size, however, give some indication of the difficulties involved in establishing any kind of record in a field in which exaggeration seems to be a sport in its own right. The most convincing and authoritative account is undoubtedly that given by our old friend Frank Buckland, who, under the heading MONSTER SALMON FROM THE TAY, gave the following details in the periodical *Land and Water* on 25th June 1870.

Mr Charles, of Arabella Row, has kindly sent me word (June,

1870), that he had purchased at Billingsgate a very large
salmon, and that he wished me to examine it. I have seen
many big salmon, but never saw such a fine 'beast'—as the
Scotch fishermen call a salmon—as our friend from the Tay.
He had been caught in the nets of my friend, Mr Alexander
Speedie, the energetic and well-known tacksman, of Perth.
Mr Speedie writes me that his men caught the fish on the
Haggis fishing-bank, about two miles below Newburg, on the
Tay. Wishing to be certain of the weight of this Tay fish, Mr
Charles was good enough to put him on the scales in my
presence. He was within an ounce or two of *seventy pounds*, and
he would have turned the scale at this weight, only from
exposure on the slab he had become somewhat dry, and
therefore lost a little of his weight. I measured him carefully.
His total length from tip of nose to edge of tail was 4ft 5in; his
girth, 2ft 7½in; and length of head, 12in. Reader, chalk or
pencil out these measurements, and you will see what a
wonderful fish this was, and he was as handsome as he was
bulky. The wholesale price was over £9. I took up the fish to
Albany Street. I soon had him under the plaster, and before
dark I got a very fair mould of this king of fishes. I then took
him back again to sleep in the ice in Mr Charles' shop. I did not
injure a scale with the casting process, and he tumbled out of his
mould like a great bullock.

P. D. Malloch, in *Life History and Habits of the Salmon, Sea-trout and
Other Freshwater Fish*, while corroborating the details about the
dimensions of the fish, the place it was captured and the captor (he
even mentions Buckland's cast), then proceeds to cloud the issue
entirely by stating quite categorically that the year was 1872 and
that the fish weighed 71 lb, remarking that it had 'evidently lost

The celebrated fish caught in the nets of Alexander Speedie on the
Tay in June 1870. Its weight is variously given as 70 lb, 71 lb and
74 lb. The first of these is probably the most reliable.

1 1 b by the time it reached London, as I distinctly remember seeing
it in Mr Speedie's window in Perth, labelled 71 lb'. He also
reproduced a photograph of the fish.

By the time we come across the Hon. A. E. Gathorne Hardy's
account in the salmon volume in the *Fur, Feather and Fin* series, we
find the fish has swollen to 74 lb (though he does admit that it
weighed 70 lb in London 'the next day', which does not give it very
long to have lingered in Mr Speedie's window), and better and
better, that it is the very same fish that Dr Browne, the Bishop of
Bristol, lost on 'the last night but one of the rod season of 1868' after
a ten and a half hour battle. The good Bishop identified the fish 'by a
mark where he had seen the tail hook of the minnow when the fish
showed itself, and a peculiarity of the firm of the shoulder'.

Just to show what can happen to facts in a good fishing story it is worth noting that by 1945, when A. Courtney Williams got hold of the story and wrote about it in *Angling Diversions*, the weight of the fish was back to 71 lb, the year was 1871 and the fish had shrunk in length by an inch. In addition, the Bishop's minnow, which in 1868 had pulled loose at the very last moment minus the hooks, was firmly back in the monster's jaws.

I believe Frank Buckland. I am also perfectly willing to accept his addition of an ounce or two to tip the scales at 70 lb, and am only surprised that he did not lean on them a little himself just to make certain.

For the world record Atlantic salmon we have to go to Norway, where in July 1928 a fish weighing 79.38 lb was caught on rod and line in the Tana by a postmaster, one Henrik Henriksen. In fact, in the 1920s, Norway yielded a number of colossal fish. In 1921 there were two from the Aarø weighing $69\frac{1}{2}$ lb and $68\frac{1}{4}$ lb respectively, in 1922 one of 69.67 lb from the Evanger and in 1924 another of $69\frac{1}{2}$ lb from the Namsen. By comparison, there are no trustworthy records of British fish caught on a rod and line weighing more than Miss Ballantine's celebrated 64-pounder from the Tay. There is, however, a delightful story concerning a salmon caught by a ghillie on the Earl of Home's beat on the Tweed which one would like to believe.

Apparently, after one particularly long day on the river, the Earl's fishing guests retired to enjoy the warm aprés fishing hospitality at The Hirsel but, as the light had not yet gone completely, the ghillie, Jimmy Scott, decided to have a cast or two on his own account. It was his first week on the river.

After only a few casts he hooked what he was later to decribe as a 'great black sow' of a fish. Several times in the gathering dusk he saw the back of the monster salmon show above the water before plunging again into a deep pool.

The Tweed was running low and Jimmy Scott conceived the idea that if he could cross to the far bank in the shallows below the pool, a length of shelving gravel might offer the best opportunity of beaching the fish.

Alas, poor Jimmy, not yet fully acquainted with the often treacherous river bed of the Tweed, achieved the crossing without realising that at the same time he had put a razor-sharp edge of rock between himself and the fish. Inevitably it broke his cast.

He continued as ghillie to successive Earls of Home for sixty years and never made the same mistake again!

After this disaster, Jimmy spent a sleepless night and the following morning was at the waterside at first light to look again on the scene of his Waterloo. Then he caught sight of the white underbelly of a fish floating just below the pool. Yes, it was his 'great black sow'. Jimmy had been fishing with two flies on his cast, a more common practice in those days than it is now. His fish had taken the bottom fly and in his dash for freedom the top one had got caught up on an underwater log. One feels the gallant monster deserved a better fate. It weighed 74 lb, but when Jimmy recounted the circumstances of its capture to the Laird it was simply entered in the game book as one of the six fish caught that day with 'largest 74 lb', without further comment in the remarks column. Lord Home did not consider it to be a fish which had been taken fairly.

The Earls of Home are associated more directly with other record-breaking fish, of which the best known is one of 69¾ lb taken by one the Earls in the eighteenth or early nineteenth century (as far as the date is concerned, Ashley Cooper states 1743, and Calderwood quotes a letter dated 1835), and another one weighing 61 lb caught by William, Earl of Home, who died in 1760. But there is so much unknown about the date and method of capture, let alone the accuracy of the scales, that these fish inevitably have to be placed on a par with Jimmy Scott's.

The great difficulty with salmon records is that many of the largest fish were, as with the Earls of Home, caught so long ago that all evidence of their existence has disappeared. What are we to make of the 67 lb fish caught on rod and line in 1812 on the River Nith at Barjarg by Jock Wallace, a notorious poacher? It was hooked at eight in the morning and landed at six in the evening, by which time only two strands of Jock's plaited hair line were left to prevent it regaining its freedom. Apparently, after landing it was taken to Barjarg Tower to be weighed, whereupon a certificate attesting to its size was signed by witnesses. What has happened to the certificate?

This catalogue of potentially record-breaking salmon makes one thing clear. The official rod-caught record represents merely the most fully documented fish. Larger salmon have, in all probability, been landed, and certainly hooked and lost. In 1908 P. D. Malloch wrote, in a rather off-hand manner:

> Fish between 50 and 60 lb in weight are often caught in the nets on the Tay, while a few between 60 and 65 lb are sometimes captured; but beyond this weight fish are rare. I have noticed in our fish-house as many as forty fish over 40 lb in weight, all caught in one day with the nets. In smaller rivers, however, a 40 lb fish is considered a monster . . . the average weight of the heaviest salmon taken with the nets each year on the Tay for fourteen years is 60 lb 2 oz.

And so to Miss Ballantine's record fish. Oddly enough, like Jimmy Scott's Tweed salmon, it too was caught on a fishing sortie by a

Harling on the Tay above Dunkeld a few miles upstream from where
Miss Ballantine caught her record 64 lb salmon in 1922.

ghillie, though in this case it was the ghillie's daughter who held the
rod. But perhaps this is not odd at all, for ghillies surely have more
opportunity and in all probability a great deal more skill than most
of us.

On this particular occasion, the head boatman on the
Glendelvine beat of the Tay was asked to 'fish for the house' as the
Laird had a headache. This was quite a usual practice. Few Lairds

67

would lie happy in bed with the fish running up. Perish the thought that the next day 'his' might be providing sport for his neighbour up river. Glendelvine was the family home of the Lyle family, as it still happily remains. Mr (later Sir) Alexander Lyle had the quite admirable habit of recording interesting events in his daily life, which he had privately printed in a series of small books for his family and friends.

Of the capture of the muckle fish of Glendelvine he wisely allowed Miss Ballantine, the boatman's daughter, to tell the story in her own words.

'This led me (wrote Mr Lyle) to ask Miss Ballantine to write out the true story of the great fish-fight, as she was now the only one living who knew all that could be known about it and who, moreover, from letters I had at various times received, possessed, I knew a very graphic pen and could tell it well. It is given below in her own words.'

I can only endorse Mr Lyle's judgement. So far as I know, Miss Ballantine's own account has not been published before and I am grateful to Sir Gavin Lyle of Glendelvine for allowing me to do so now.

LANDING OF THE RECORD TAY SALMON
7th OCTOBER 1922

'Are you there? Hurry up, you will have to fill a vacancy to-day; there is a message from Glendelvine to say that the Laird won't be down.'

Feverishly the household duties were performed that morning, and as I raced up the river bank to join the boat, how I blessed the Laird for having a headache!

A whole day's fishing, a glorious, sunny, autumn day, how I rejoiced to be alive. But such feelings only an angler can understand. To some, the uncertainty of fishing constitutes its chief attraction: to others, the fascination lies in the solitude of the surroundings, the fragrance and beauty of the woods, the songs of the birds, and the enchantment of running water.

And what of the boatmen? One thing is certain, that a good deal of the angler's success or failure depends on the efficiency of the men at the oars. The oarsman that day was one of the finest anglers who ever cast a salmon line on the waters of the mighty Tay—my father—but who, alas, will cast no more. In addition to him was Melvin, who is blind of an eye and takes size nine boots.

At tea-time we returned home with three salmon, and as the clock would go back one hour that night, and fishing days were nearing an end, we decided to continue till dusk. Melvin knocked off, father and I refreshed ourselves with tea, and . leisurely towed the boat to the top of the Boat Pool, a favourite haunt, where the stream is rapid and the current broken.

As is customary when harling, two rods were used, the fly 'Wilkinson' on right, and the dace which I plyed on left. We swung out as the October sun hung low over Birnam Hill, and a few turns at the top brought no result. As the last rays of the great crimson ball shone direct in the eyes of the fish there came a draw upon the line which I was plying, a sharp strike, and connection was established.

Then began an Homeric battle. He was hooked well out in the stream above the Bargie Stone, and after a few seconds of very ordinary play, we decided to land him at the broken bank, behind Bargie, on the Murthly side, the slack water there being an advantage.

But the fish's plan and ours did not coincide. Whir-r-r! An alarming amount of the line was torn off, the reel screeched as it had never screeched before, the fish careered madly down-stream, leaving only a whirl of spray in its train. Within the fraction of a second the boat was turned down-stream, and down, down, following hard on the heels of the fish, we were compelled to go. After this first furious rush—about 500 yards—he lost his bearings, and came to a sudden halt close to the north bank, and about 100 yards above the bridge. By that time, however, I had retrieved all the slack line, and had him well under hand, though my arm ached desperately and my left forefinger was cut in an effort to check the line. Here we were in the act of landing, when the fish rolled in to the end of the boat, thus offering an opportunity for gaffing. Had a third party been at hand to hold the boat, the fish undoubtedly would have been gaffed in the space of ten minutes.

Without delay he righted himself, and sailed off majesti-cally into the deep, ever after that showing a marked disinclination to come to close quarters. He again elected to go down-stream, and ran out in a line with the North Pier of the bridge.

A moment of frightful anxiety followed when he threat-ened to go through between the piers. But he chose to favour us, and the bridge was safely negotiated.

We were now out of the boat, and following the fish, he, meanwhile, keeping about twenty yards from the bank, but showing a tendency to get further out into the current.

Twilight was fading fast, so father thought it wise to run back and fetch the boat, while I hung on to the 'refractory beast', who kept advancing and retiring at intervals, but inclining always downstream.

Again boarding the boat we endeavoured to get round to his other side, but that seemed only to spur him on to further effort, and though we worked with him for fully half an hour in mid-stream, he showed no signs of weariness. Then he settled down to intervals of sulking, giving an occasional dive and shake of his head. This period was a steady solid fight for victory between man and monster.

I suggested pelting him with the stones in the boat, but got short cuttings—'Na, na, we'll try nane o' thae capers!' Eventually we manoeuvred him to the opposite side, where, in the darkness, the trees of the island stood silhouetted against the sky, and where it now seemed as if we were destined to spend the night.

Tiring of sulking, the fish began to jag, each jag running like an electric shock down my spine. What language can describe the phases we passed through in that hour; apprehension, hope, and deadly fear. Would the line hold? Was the cast frayed? Was the fish lightly hooked? Would the rod top straighten out if a heavier strain was put on?

Unspoken thoughts such as these passed through our minds. Victory—or failure—was at hand, the next few minutes would see us the happiest or most miserable of human beings.

Though utterly exhausted, sheer determination kept me from giving up the rod, as tighter and tighter still came the order, and nearer and nearer came our quarry. By changing my seat to the bow of the boat, and keeping the rod in an upright position, father was enabled to feel with the gaff the knot at the junction of line and cast. Gauging the distance by the length of the cast ($3\frac{3}{4}$ yards), the stroke was delivered, and a wriggling monster was heaved over the seat into the floor of the boat, vigorously flapping his tail.

Again, what eloquence could do justice to such a moment

in one's life? Better left to be imagined.

He was hooked half a mile further up the river at 6.15; it was now 8.20: two hours and five minutes of nerve-racking anxiety, thrilling excitement, and good stiff work. One thing was decidedly in our favour, we were mercifully ignorant of the size of the fish. From start to finish he never showed himself above the surface. That he was hefty we could well judge from his weight and movements, but nothing more than 35–40 lbs was anticipated. He proved to be the heaviest fish of the season, the fish of many seasons, the record for the British Isles.

As we had no spring balance capable of coping with the fish's weight, two passers-by were hailed to carry the 'beast', slung on a pole, to Boatlands Farm, where, in the presence of a number of people, it was carefully weighed on a tested steelyard, half an hour after capture. Though slightly copper-coloured, the fish was in good condition and fresh run, as sea lice were found still adhering to its tail.

It was gifted to Perth Royal Infirmary by Mr Lyle, where it was relished by both patients and staff.

A cast was made by P. D. Malloch, and now the fish displays its lordly proportions at the Mansion House of Glendelvine, where it is looked upon as one of the sporting treasures. An expert's reading of the scales showed that the salmon had not spawned previously, had spent two years in fresh water as a parr, three years in the sea, and would have been six years old in 1923.

Details and Measurements
Captured in 'Boat Pool,' Glendelvine Water, 7.10.22.

Size of river	3 feet on bridge gauge.
Male fish	64 lbs.

Big Fish

Length	54 inches.
Girth	28½ inches.
Head	12 inches.
Tail	11 inches.

Day's catch—64, 25, 21, 17 total 127 lbs.

Miss Ballantine was eighteen years old when she caught her remarkable fish.

Travellers from Perth on the Caputh road, when they cross the iron bridge over the Tay, might pause a moment to gaze at the scene of the epic struggle. The Bargie Stone where the fish was hooked is only a short distance upstream on the left bank, whilst the cottage where Miss Ballantine spent the rest of her days stands hard by the waterside on the other bank. In later years she was crippled with arthritis but insisted that she be wheeled each day into the porch of her cottage from where she could gaze at the scene of her triumph.

Without in any way detracting from her achievement, it should be made clear that almost as much credit must go to her father as to Miss Ballantine herself. On big rivers such as the Tay where the water can only be covered properly from a boat, it is entirely the boatman's skill and intimate knowledge of where the fish are most likely to be lying which leads to success. An experienced boatman will know the contours of the river bed as exactly as if it were dry land. The fisherman has little to do but sit and allow the boatman to manoeuvre his bait over likely lies—a form of fishing known as harling.

The account of how the record fish was gaffed is also remarkable. To have been able to locate the knot at the end of the line underwater, in pitch darkness, and then gaff the fish cleanly, when it must have been around five feet below the surface, was a

73

fine piece of work indeed.

As the discerning reader will have noticed, Miss Ballantine's salmon was caught on a 'dace'. This, incidentally, does not refer to the coarse fish of that name, but to a type of old-fashioned brownish spinner. It was at any rate not a fly. For that record we have to go to the River Deveron.

Like almost every other big salmon, this was a cock fish caught in the 'back end' of the year, on 21st October 1924, to be precise, by a Mrs Morison, fishing from the bank using a $1\frac{1}{4}$ in. fly on the Montblairy beat of the Deveron. When it was weighed twenty-four hours after its capture it tipped the scales at 61 lb, and it is often claimed that it would have weighed 62 lb at the time it was landed. 'Tiny' Morison was a very fine fisherman indeed, but her husband, Captain Morison, was in a class of his own. Yet he never caught a fish of over 40 lb in his life: 40 lb, incidentally, being the normally accepted minimum weight for the 'big fish' category, or what our grandfathers called 'portmanteaux' fish. For the purposes of this chapter, however, I have increased the pass mark to 60 lb, for although most fishermen, like Captain Morison, never have the good fortune to tangle with a 40-pounder, there are too many records and stories about fish at this weight to include in anything smaller than an encyclopaedia. What, for example, is one to make of Mrs Radclyffe, fishing in September 1924 on the Lower Scone beat of the Tay, who killed *in one day* on the same fly (a Silver Wilkinson) three fish weighing 42, 41 and 18 lb respectively?

At this stage it seems appropriate to wonder if there is any truth in the frequently repeated suggestion that fisher*women* are a great deal luckier than fisher*men*. Of course, there is an element of luck in fishing. Over a given period a good fisherman will always catch more fish than a bad one, but I have witnessed enough incidents when men have had their eyes wiped by 'mere women' to wonder

A 40 lb or 'Portmanteau' fish. The champagne cork used as a bung for
the gaff adds a jubilant note.

whether the Big Fisherman in the Sky looks upon the female of the species with an especially kindly eye.

I can recall one particularly cold morning when four fishermen had toiled unsuccessfully for several hours on the Ballathie beat on the Tay.

On returning to the fishing hut for luncheon one of the fisherman's wives who had been huddled cosily round the stove asked her husband if she could have a cast to which he benignly agreed.

Now he was spinning with the latest of modern reels which are essentially easy enough to handle but do require, when making a cast, that the fisherman should press a release catch so that the line may be allowed to run free.

This was patiently explained to the lady who had never fished in her life before. Alas, in the excitement of the moment she overlooked this slight but important formality so that when she made her cast the Devon minnow splashed into the water a matter of a yard from her feet.

Of course, everybody fell about laughing at this evidence of female incompetence but were abruptly silenced when there was a very large splash indeed and a splendid fish attached itself firmly to the hook. The lady then proceeded to play it with commendable cool and upon landing it remarked that salmon fishing seemed to be a fairly easy matter. Understandably a great cloud of gloom descended on all the gentlemen present.

On another occasion a fishing party broke off to partake of a picnic on the bank. The only lady who had been fishing, instead of reeling in her line and laying aside her rod in the proper manner, left it where she had been fishing with the line trailing in the water.

Yes, exactly! When she had done justice to an excellent meal she wandered back to the bank and picked up her rod to find that she had a salmon obligingly waiting for her on the end of her line.

And so the stories of lucky lady fishermen go on. I know someone who claims that the only fish caught at the end of an otherwise blank day was when the family nanny, relieved temporarily of her charges when the disconsolate party retired to the fishing hut, wandered off downstream with a rod and came back with *three* fish which she landed unaided. The next day, which had also been blank, she was challenged to repeat the feat but this time only caught two! It is needless to relate that she had never fished before.

So where does that leave Miss Ballantine and Mrs Morison? Pure coincidence or just another example of the luck of the ladies?

Would you believe that the rod-caught record for England and Wales this century, and for any *spring* fish, is a salmon weighing $59\frac{1}{2}$ lb caught in the Wye on 13 March 1923 by *Miss* Doreen Davey? Jock Scott, in his fascinating compilation of heavy fish, *Game Fish Records*, notes that it was landed after a long struggle in the dark by the light of bonfires!

Incidentally, the Wye, particularly in the 1920s, was noted for the number of big fish caught or, as in the case of one particular giant, found dead and too decomposed to make an accurate estimation of its live weight. It measured $59\frac{1}{2}$ in. long and was 33 in. in girth, compared to Miss Ballantine's 54 by $28\frac{1}{2}$ in. fish caught two years later. The Wye fish still had an artificial minnow in its mouth. It is perhaps fortunate that the unlucky fisherman never knew just how big the one was that got away.

Whether these records will ever be broken seems, at the moment, unlikely. Yet, just as the size of autumn and spring runs fluctuates over the years, so too the average size of the fish vary from year to year, or decade to decade. The 1920s seems to have been a decade of large fish, but quite why that should have been is hard to say. Today, netting stations off the river mouths report that, whilst some big fish are still caught, the average weight is falling. On the Tay, for example, Malloch's commonplace 40-pounders are rarely to be seen. Perhaps the size of salmon runs in cycles and we shall see again those splendid letters to the *Field* describing day-long battles with giant fish which threw the hook at the very point of the gaff.

VERY DISGUSTING

THE GHILLIE

'Treat your ghillie like a human being; some anglers are strangely inconsistent in this important matter.'

Jock Scott, 1933

Of all the many and varied characters engaged in the pursuits of the countryside surely as a class the ghillie must hold a pre-eminent place.

There are, of course, many memorable names engaged in other sports who have left their footprints in history; some have even become immortalised in song like John Peel with his coat so grey or in legend like John Brown, Queen Victoria's personal servant and hill keeper. There are few families of longstanding who have not had outdoor servants, whether gamekeepers, stalkers, grooms or gardeners, who have not become part of the family tapestry, remembered with affection and, not infrequently by younger members of the family, with considerable awe.

Perhaps the reason why ghillies as a class are so often of this category is that of all employees they have the opportunity of coming into the closest contact with the employers. Much of a gamekeeper's life, for example, is spent keeping his lonely vigil over his precious game birds, and it is only when shoots are being planned or prospects for the season being discussed, that he sees much of his master.

79

George Walby, who worked as a ghillie on the lower Wye for
more than 50 years, with his home-made gaff.

The ghillie on the river, however, during the long fishing season
is a daily companion, mentor and familiar friend. The river is his
kingdom and the fishing hut his castle.

'Ma Gawd, ma Gawd, the deescipline is a awa tae hell the day!
Put doon yer whusky yer Grace and get the lot o' ye doon the
watter.' As I once heard a head ghillie admonish his ducal master
when an over-protracted luncheon seemed in prospect.

Auld Rob o' the Trews, a splendid portrait of whom appears on
the cover of this book, was one of the ghillies in the great tradition.

The Ghillie

Sir Herbert Maxwell, who in 1905 wrote *The Story of the Tweed*, described him as 'a very Prince among Tweed Boatmen', high praise indeed for a boatman on a river, perhaps above all rivers, noted for great characters.

Auld Rob was born Robert Kerss in 1779 and spent his whole working life on the Tweed in the service of Sir Thomas Macdougall Brisbane, Bt, and Lady Macdougall of Makerstoun.

The portrait was done by Robert Frain a much neglected Scottish painter who, like his contemporary Raeburn, specialised in painting the gentry of his time—a rare tribute to Rob in that it is unusual for a family servant to have the distinction of being painted full length in oils. The picture has since been widely copied in lithographs and engravings.

Rob's clothing with his billycock hat, adorned with salmon flies, is unusually old-fashioned even for his time, but the sturdy wooden rowing boat in the background is identical with many used on the Tweed to this day.

The picture itself was lost for many years and turned up on Merseyside in 1934 when, through the good offices of Mr William Morris of London, it was returned to Makerstoun where it was given pride of place above the sideboard in the dining-room. A fortunate choice as in a disastrous fire in 1970, the centuries-old stone vaulted dining-room was one of the few rooms to escape complete destruction. It then spent five years in storage in Edinburgh before being cleaned and returned to the rebuilt Makerstoun, still occupied by a descendant of the original family.

Of the many anecdotes about Rob of the Trews handed down from generation to generation, one in particular demonstrates something of the independence of character of the grand old man.

One very cold day Rob was rowing a gentleman who hooked a fish. Rob rowed ashore, landed the fish and the gentleman refreshed himself from his hip flask. This happened three times. The last time, instead of getting back into the boat, Rob sauntered away—the gentleman called out, 'Rob, Rob, where are you going ?' Whereupon Rob replied, 'Them that drinks by theirsels, can fush by theirsels,' and stomped off home.

The partiality for a dram of so many ghillies is proverbial.

There is a splendid story of an Irish ghillie who had attended an American gentleman all day whilst he lashed the water unsuccessfully in driving rain. The American applied himself repeatedly to his whisky flask without offering it to his retainer.

Finally, trying to light a cigarette, he found his matchbox water-logged.

'Is there no dry place on this damn river where I can strike a match,' he complained.

'Ye could try the back of me throat,' replied the ghillie sourly.

Then there is the sad story of a ghillie on one of the finer beats of the Aberdeenshire Dee. Venerable in years, he had served the same master faithfully and well all his lifetime, beloved by family and fishing guests alike.

It was only a short time before he was due to retire that he appeared to undergo something of a personality change. Whereas he had always shown considerable disapproval of any tendency for the rods to linger overlong in the luncheon hut, he now took to staying behind to 'clear up'.

At first this was put down to his advancing years, until the evidence became more and more unmistakable. When he returned to his duties, he was noticeably unsteady. At risk of making this true account less than believable, it has to be reported that the symptoms became so marked that on one occasion, when attempting to gaff a fish, he finished up alongside it in the water which was deep and fast-flowing. Perhaps, fortunately, he had a cork leg, a relic of the 1914–18 War, which enabled the master to then gaff his ghillie and pull him to safety without inflicting too much damage. But, of course, it was a situation which could not continue.

The odd thing was that the ample stocks of alcohol kept in the fishing hut did not appear to be declining with any greater rapidity than usual. It was only when it was noticed that the brass-work in the hut, such as the door knobs, had begun to show signs of neglect, together with the discovery of a cache of empty Brasso tins, that the truth dawned. Two fingers of Brasso, even when mixed with an equal quantity of water, is not a recipe for sobriety.

Retired, only slightly prematurely, it is good to be able to report that he lived on happily for many more years under the eagle eye of his wife who set out his dram for him every day and kept the key of the pantry down the front of her ample bosom.

In contrast, there was another Deeside ghillie who is still remembered for quite different reasons.

Leekie ruled 'his' stretch of the Dee, just below Ballater, for over forty years. He was a man of perfect manners and bearing. Each morning he would arrive at the riverside resplendent in perfectly cut plus-fours, his boots burnished to the standard of the Brigade of Guards, and his handlebar moustache oiled and gleaming. He disdained to wear waders but, should it be required in order to gaff a fish, he would stride into the water up to his waist without hesitation. After the hardest of days fishing, he would reappear the following morning exactly at the appointed time as immaculately turned out as ever.

Leekie's indifference to getting his feet wet is in marked contrast to some others of his kind. The late Lord Londonderry's Irish ghillie of many years, Billy Flynn, not only had a marked aversion to water and would seldom venture into even the shallowest edge

The traditional ghillie has always been a staunch supporter . . .

. . . discreet adviser . . .

. . . trusting anchor . . .

. . . and is prepared to take on any role in the interests of his rod's
sport.

but would panic if his employer did so, prophesying that he would undoubtedly be swept away.

An odd weakness in an otherwise splendid character and perhaps explainable by the fact that in common with a surprising number of ghillies and boatmen he could not swim.

Consider, however, by contrast this passage from William Scrope's *Days and Nights of Salmon Fishing in the Tweed* (1843):

Wading in the water is not only an agreeable thing in itself, but absolutely necessary in some rivers in the North that are destitute of boats; and that you may do this in the best possible style, procure half a dozen pair of shoes, with large knob-nails at some distance asunder: if they are too close, they will bring your foot to an even surface, and it will glide off a stone or rock, which in deep water may be inconvenient. Cut some holes in the upper-leathers of your shoes, to give the water a free passage out of them when you are on dry land; not because the fluid is annoying, for we should wrong you to say so, but to prevent the pumping noise you would otherwise make at every step. If you are not much of a triton, you may use fishermen's boots, and keep yourself dry: it is all a matter of taste. When you are wading through the rapids, step on quickly and boldly, and do not gaze down on the stream after the fashion of Narcissus; for running waves will not reflect your beauty, but only make your head giddy. If you stop for a moment, place your legs abreast of each other: should you fancy a straddle, with one of them in advance, the action of the water will operate upon both, trip you up, and carry you out to sea. Observe, I am talking of a heavy stream. The body of a man, who probably lost his life in this manner, was found low down the river when I was fishing. I asked John Haliburton, who

86

was then my fisherman, where it came from. 'I suppose,' said he, 'it travelled all the way from Peebles.' (Note: Peebles was about twenty-five miles from the spot in question.)

Avoid standing upon rocking stones, for obvious reasons; and never go into the water deeper than the fifth button of your waistcoat: even this does not always agree with tender constitutions in frosty weather. As you are likely not to take a just estimate of the cold in the excitement of the sport, should you be of a delicate temperament, and be wading in the month of February, when it may chance to freeze very hard, pull down your stockings, and examine your legs. Should they be black, or even purple, it might, perhaps, be as well to get on dry land; but if they are only rubicund, you may continue to enjoy the water, if it so pleases you.

As has been remarked in the previous chapter on fishing flies, confidence is one of the more important weapons in a fisherman's armoury, and to have a good ghillie in attendance is perhaps the greatest confidence builder of all.

He is a foolish fellow, indeed, who, having taken an expensive beat for a week or two, does not heed the advice of the ghillie or boatman. Most ghillies have spent a lifetime on the river and most likely also their fathers before them.

One such family relationship was of a rather different nature. A highly respected ghillie who, happily, although getting on in years, is still very much with us today, went to spend his holidays with his uncle who happened to be the village schoolmaster and, therefore, a person of some standing in the community.

He was also a regular attender at the village tavern where he spent many convivial hours in the company of his cronies whilst, unknown to all but a select few, his nephew of about ten years of age was standing up to his middle in the river nearby tending the schoolmaster's net. His job was rather like that of a linesman at Wimbledon who keeps his finger on the cord to detect a net ball. Whenever the lad felt a salmon hit the net, he would run to the inn and tap his finger on the window whereupon the schoolmaster would excuse himself, dispatch the netted fish and conceal it before returning to his libations.

It is to be hoped that it was the reprehensible behaviour of his uncle that persuaded the young lad to go straight and join the forces of law and order in later life.

The ghillie's is a profession in which tradition is strong and few acquire the knowledge and wisdom to make a success of the job who do not start young. Even if their earliest experiences, like those of the dominie's nephew, were not strictly legal.

A. E. Knox, who fished and wrote about fishing particularly on the River Spey over a hundred years ago, is probably now less remembered than his ghillie. Here is Knox's own account, written in 1874, of how the partnership started.

My first experience of him was at the commencement of the previous season. He was then a little boy about twelve years of age, and hardly strong enough, or tall enough, as I fancied, to gaff a large salmon, or wade after me into deep water, as would occasionally be necessary. But there was something very promising about him. He was remarkably quiet and taciturn, and although at first a little awkward, yet, before a month had elapsed, I found that, from his natural intelligence, his love of the sport, and his amphibious habits, [*sic*] he possessed, in embryo, all the qualifications of a perfect aquatic gillie. He soon became an adept with the clip, seldom missing when he had a fair chance, and rarely throwing one away;

while to his coolness and presence of mind in moments of difficulty, during a long and exciting run, I have since frequently been indebted for the successful capture of many a heavy fish. This was the beginning of Simon's second season as my attendant.

Little could Knox have known for how many years he would remain 'indebted'. Simon long outlived him to become yet another legendary figure.

Incidentally, the name 'clip' for a gaff, although I have not heard it now for many years, is, I believe, still current in certain parts and its operator in consequence known as a 'clipper'.

Apart from the advice which most ghillies will readily offer, it is frequently their skill with the gaff or net which decides the outcome of a hard-fought contest.

In this context, perhaps Her Majesty The Queen Mother, an extremely expert salmon fisher, will forgive my retelling this story.

She hooked a salmon, which was brought to the gaff without undue difficulty, and successfully landed. Her attendant unhooked the fish and threw it up the bank before turning to attend to the Queen Mother's rod.

At this point, the fish took matters into its own hands and managed to contrive to flop back into the water before the horrified gaze of the ghillie. As if to celebrate its unexpected freedom, the fish then rose out of the water in a sort of victory roll whereupon the ghillie, with a deft stroke of the clip, returned it safely to the bank where it was quickly dispatched.

'Goodness. I've never seen that done before' Her Majesty is alleged to have remarked imperturbably.

Undoubtedly she was served by what in early days was known as a 'clever clipper'.

The Queen Mother, then the Duchess of York, confers with a ghillie
on her way to the next pool.

The Royal Family's love of fishing is well known and there are
several, probably apochryphal stories told as much to the
amusement of the Royal Family as anyone else.

There is one which I would dearly like to be true.

The story goes that the Queen was fishing from one bank of a
broad river when a lady, in breast high waders, was casting away
from the far bank.

Suddenly, she became aware that the figure opposite her was
none other than Her Majesty. It was a situation not envisaged in
any known book on etiquette and the unfortunate lady decided
that the correct course was to attempt a curtsey.

Unfortunately, in doing so, she managed to ship a large

quantity of very cold water into her waders and she was last seen floating gently downstream.

The tradition amongst the Royal Family of being keen (and generally expert) salmon fishermen goes back as far as George IV. He was the first of the Hanoverian monarchs to visit Scotland—a visit that is still keenly remembered if mainly because of his startling appearance at his first levee at Holyrood Palace in full Highland dress worn over startling pink tights designed to keep the Royal legs warm.

Little is known of his fishing exploits other than that he was considered competent, and that the Coachman fly was created for him by the Royal coachman.

King George V's activities at the waterside have been more widely if not always quite accurately reported.

Here is the literal translation quoted in a book by Sir George Aston, written around 1921, of an article by a French journalist. It appeared during the Great War with the admirable intention of improving the King's image with our allies.

He is an angler of the first force, the King of Britain. Behold him there as he sits motionless under his umbrella, patiently regarding his many-coloured floats. How obstinately he contends with the elements! It is a summer day in Britain, that is to say a day of sleet and fog and tempest. But, what would you? It is as they love it, those who follow the sport.

Presently, the King's float begins to descend. My God! But how he strikes! The hook is implanted in the very bowels of the salmon. The King rises. He spurns aside his footstool. He strides strongly and swiftly towards the rear. In good time the salmon comes to approach himself to the bank. Aha! The King has cast aside his rod. He hurls himself flat on the ground

LOCH TAY—(*February*)
Having fixed his rod, he now takes forty winks.

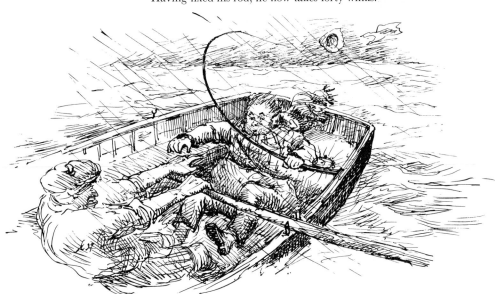

And is roused by a kick from the boatman, and the rush of a thirty-
pounder.

on his victim. They splash and struggle in the icy water. Name of a dog! But it is a 'braw laddie'!

The ghillie, a kind of outdoor domestic, administers the *coup de grâce* with his pistol. The King cries with a very shrill voice 'Hip, hip, hurrah!' On these red-letter days His Majesty King George dines on a haggis and a whisky grog. Like a true Scotsman, he wears only a kilt.

It is understandable perhaps that ghillies as a breed tend to adopt the stern expression of disapproval more appropriate to a church elder. In these days when so many fishings are syndicated resulting in a succession of 'unknown quantities' passing through his hands, his uncompromising gravity on first meeting the new rods for a week or longer is a defensive guard against an unseemly familiarity, rather after the practice of a schoolmaster taking charge of a new form. Unless he asserts his authority at the outset, all is lost.

Once the fisherman has demonstrated that he will bow to his superior knowledge, take his advice and not treat him as a hired servant, the thaw sets in so that he sees him depart with regret and looks forward to the possibility of his return.

Equally, whilst the average ghillie is quick to recognise and respect the ability of an experienced fisherman, he is patience itself with a self-confessed duffer.

I once arranged for an American friend of mine to be taken out by a very experienced, if somewhat dour, boatman. Now the American was an expert who took his fishing very seriously indeed. He was one of the finest fly casters I have ever seen and after the American custom fished with the very shortest of rods and the lightest of tackle.

Willie, the ghillie, regarded all this with the deepest suspicion but, when shortly after the start the American not only hooked a good fish but brought it expertly to the net, the air of distant disapproval started to dissipate.

'A fine fush Sorr,' said Willie, holding it up for inspection.

The American nodded absently.

'Throw it back,' he said.

For a moment for Willie the whole world stood still. Never in his life had he heard anything so profane.

'I only keep fish over 30 pounds,' said the American, casually, and prepared to resume fishing.

Slowly Willie lowered the fish back into the water and applied himself again to the oars in a silence as deep as the Grand Canyon. The American caught two more fish, neither of which came up to the required weight and were duly returned to the water.

At the end of the day, Willie declined a more than generous tip and that night got drunk on his own money. Sacrilege had been committed.

By contrast another American who came under Willie's care was inept to a degree almost impossible to imagine even for a beginner.

His line was in a constant tangle, he snagged the bottom of the river and got hooked up on every tree in sight.

Then, against all the odds, he hooked a fish. It made a sharp dive and within seconds had broken. The American reeled in and examined the end of his cast now bereft of the fly.

'Did you see that,' he exclaimed incredulously. 'That Goddamn salmon has just chewed the bug off the end of my string!'

From that moment on Willie was his devoted slave.

Such is the stuff of which ghillies are made.

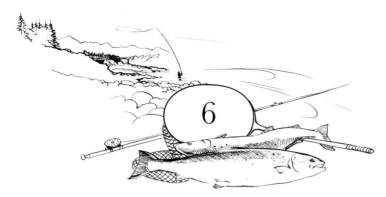

THE GENTLE ART OF
POACHING

*'Right glad I am to do ye a favour, ye shall no want for a salmon whilst I
have one.' So saying, he pulled forth a ten pounder, which occupied all
the lower regions of his jacket. 'How the beast got here,' said he, as he
extracted him gradually, 'I dinna ken, but I am thinking that he must
have louped intill my pocket, as I war wading the river.'*

William Scrope, 1843

The poacher, whether he appropriates the odd brace of pheasants
from the landlord's coverts, takes a stag off the hill or a salmon from
the river, is traditionally regarded with a measure of amused
affection by country folk. Even his sworn enemy the gamekeeper
has been known to stand him a pint in the local ('At least a know
where the b— is when he's supping my ale'), and the landowner
himself, unless he be an uncommonly mean one, would be unlikely
to be too severe on a local caught red-handed taking 'one for the
pot'. At least this was true in the old days but not so now as will shortly
be recounted.

I have an amusing recollection of meeting a charming
Irishman in a shebeen in the wilds of Connemara.

We fell to discussing the merits of various local waters, a subject
on which he was obviously the local expert.

'If you would care to come out with me Sorr,' he said, as the whisky bottle became ever lower, 'I'll give ye a day on the foinest water ye ever did see.'

Of course I accepted with alacrity but thought to ask, as I did not know the water, whether I should need waders or not.

'When ye come fishing with me Sorr,' he said solemnly, 'ye wear running shoes.'

How was I to know that he was the most notorious poacher in a part of the world where that title is not easily won!

Up to the middle of the last century, the whole question of salmon-fishing rights were not nearly so carefully regulated as they are today. This was largely, of course, because not only, as is now generally agreed, were salmon far more numerous but because they had little commercial value.

Poaching, if indeed poaching it was, was often carried out openly. At night bands of men carrying flaming torches and armed with spears and clubs drove fish upstream into traps or nets, the whole operation being conducted with the maximum noise.

There was also the consideration that Scotland, in particular, had not yet been 'discovered' by sportsmen. There were no railways to carry shooting or fishing parties from the south in comfort and journeys by stage were onerous and exhausting. Thus owners of fine salmon beats could not attract rich tenants.

Indeed, it was not always that the riparian owner had automatic fishing rights. Landowners not interested in fishing often let the rights go by default. Others were tricked out of their rights by deceit.

One cannot help but be slightly amused by the altogether deplorable trick whereby a riparian owner was done out of his rights. It was sometime in the early nineteenth century in remote Sutherland. The main value of the salmon in those days so far as the laird was concerned, was that it provided a cheap and plentiful supply of food for feeding his large numbers of retainers and servants over whom he exercised feudal rights. Indeed, it was only after the repression of the clans after the 1745 Rebellion that a clan chief was denied the right of life and death over his clansmen. At Glamis Castle, where the Queen Mother was brought up, there is still a room known as the Hangman's Room. Indeed one of the Bowes-Lyons' house servants enjoyed the title of Hangman, although happily without exercising the role, into this century.

It happened on this particular river in Sutherland that one of the lairds coveted the salmon-fishing rights of his downstream neighbour not for sport but for the sustenance the fish provided.

On his stretch he had a small island in midstream, and happening to meet his neighbour one day, told him that he intended to build a small fort on the island and would he mind, whilst building was in progress, if his labourers could have the right of fishing the whole river until the work was complete. His unsuspecting neighbour immediately gave permission and even signed a legal document confirming the fishing and netting rights until the fort was completed. The moment this had been done, his wicked neighbour immediately stopped all work and the fishing rights remained his for many years.

On many rivers where one person owned one bank and another the other, it was customary to come to a gentleman's agreement whereby on alternate days each riparian owner had exclusive rights to fish both banks so that there was no risk of either party interfering with enjoyment of the other. Indeed, there are still many instances where this convenient and happy arrangement has continued till the present day. However, there have been several cases where one bank has changed hands the new owner, particularly where his bank provided the better fishing, has sought to overturn the arrangement. It has resulted in much bitterness and in some cases lengthy and expensive legal actions. (An alternative arrangement of dividing the water into an upper and lower beat changing over at mid-day has, on some rivers, proved more successful.)

Legislation to protect the salmon, particularly in Scotland, goes back to the earliest times.

Most of the early legislation was designed to protect the spawning salmon and the taking of them by illegal means and the penalties were severe indeed.

To quote from the introduction to W. L. Calderwood's excellent book, *The Life of the Salmon* (1908):

> From earliest times it has been considered necessary to protect spawning fish by close seasons, and to do this satisfactorily observation as to the breeding season has been inevitable. Like the crime of sheep-stealing, the crime of poaching salmon in close time was punishable by death. In the Act of the first Parliament of James I (1424) we find 'Quha sa ever be convict of slaughter of Salmonde in time forbidden be the law, he sall pay fourtie shillings for the unlaw, and at the third time, gif he be convict of sik trespasse, he sall tyne his life, or then bye it.' The transference from forty shillings (Scots) to the death penalty seens rapid nor is any indication given as to what may be regarded as the ultimate price of a poacher's life. One thing seems clear, however: those early Scottish legislators were determined to preserve the breed of salmon. God bless their memory!

Since the days of King James, however, the penalties for poaching have become progressively less onerous and poaching even to have been condoned on certain rivers by the mid-nineteenth century.

Writing on 'The Tweed and its Tributaries' Thomas Stoddart reports a veritable Armageddon:

> Such a massacre as took place near Melrose in 1846, when upwards of three hundred breeding fish writhed and bled on the prongs of a single leister, and at least six thousand, which had escaped the toils of the Berwick fishermen, and formed the hope and stay of future seasons of abundance, were cut off by means of the same deadly instrument, along the course of the river! From the effect of this bloody onslaught, Tweed has not yet recovered.

The leister is a traditional poacher's tool. Formerly more generally known as a 'waster', it is a five-pronged spear with a single barb on each prong. It is attached to a pole up to sixteen feet in length, which is around the maximum depth that fish can be spotted in clear water.

Stoddart was writing about spearing fish on the spawning redds in shallow streams where they can easily be approached in daylight. But the leister is more usually associated with a more dramatic style of poaching which took place at the dead of night. This is the famous 'art' of burning the water.

Now, burning the water has been frequently misrepresented. There is a common fallacy that if a flaming brand, or even an ordinary battery-operated torch, is held over the water, then the fish will come and investigate, whereupon they can be gaffed or speared with ease. Perhaps this is indeed the reaction of tropical fish in the Bahamas or the Seychelles, but the salmon is not so simple-minded. He either shoots off to the far end of the pool at the first sign of light, or he stays exactly where he is until he hears a splash, and then shoots off to the far end of the pool. But he is confused, just as you would be if someone shone a torch in your eyes in the middle of the night and then started to make stabs at you with a five-pronged spear.

Burning the water is a sport, or crime, that lies somewhere between otter (nowadays mink) -hunting and canoeing. It works like this.

The salmon are happily asleep in the middle of a shallow pool. The poachers using a boat or wading, or both, move into the pool. A boat is preferable because it makes less disturbance, and several boats even better because they give the fish less chance to hide. Each boat contains a minimum of three people. One to hold the torch, one to knock the fish on the head when they are in the boat, and one to wield the leister. Note that there is no oarsman. The man with the leister, punts the boat upstream, which in itself takes considerable skill in a strong current, until the light from the torch shows up the outline of a stationary salmon. One more push; the boat glides in range; the poised leister slices into the water and a flapping fish is unceremoniously dumped into the boat.

Naturally enough, the rest of the salmon head for cover. The boat follows them round the pool. A fish takes shelter behind a rock. The flickering light reveals its tail, but as the leister is raised it scuttles off under the bank. Caught by the current, the bow swings downstream rocking violently. It pivots round. A fish darts into the shallows, splashes and torpedoes back into deeper water. It halts in the lee of a shingle bank, but is spotted by the torch man. The boat glides forward and No. 2 joins his fellow under the seat in the stern. And so it goes on. The proceedings are accompanied by splashing, lurching and shouting. There are violent arguments about upsetting the boat, loud warnings of hidden rocks and frequently missed fish.

Burning the water.

The fact that burning the water is rarely carried out nowadays is not entirely due to the lack of skill of the modern poacher. It is simply absurdly easy to detect, the valuable fish are badly damaged by the leister and, alas, there are more effective methods.

The old descriptions and illustrations of burning the water make it clear that it was virtually a sport in its own right. Therein lies the charm of the traditional poacher and the reason for the frequent readiness of the proprietor or keeper to forgive and forget.

In the light of this, it might amuse here to recount a delightful story which first appeared in *Blackwood's Magazine* in 1922. It gives a highly diverting account of how matters stood between the 'gamey' and the poacher in the almost feudal days of the old Scottish estates at the turn of the century.

A hundred years or so ago, Archie MacCorquodale worked his wee croft on the edge of the moor at the top of Glen Nant. It was a hard living he scratched from the poor soil but such was Archie's nature that he would have it no other way. He was his own master except for the obligations he owned to his laird in return for the feu of his smallholding and what was the alternative? To emigrate as so many had done before him to a distant land or seek work nearer home: down the pits may be or raise his bairns in a Glasgow slum.

This bright May morning, his salmon rod tucked under his oxter, he took the hill road over the moor to the plateau which overlooks the headwaters of the River Awe.

Ten minutes later he was casting his dark-bodied fly, dressed with a heron's wing, into the peat-brown water. Step by step he worked his way down the pool expecting any moment to feel the double underwater tug and see the water boil as the hook drove home.

He was almost at the end of the broken water and about to reel in when it happened. From the way the fish took the fly smoothly and then rolled slightly to show a white flash of underbelly, he knew he had hit a big one—a really big one.

His mind concentrated on the task in hand as he backed, step by step, out of the water, and he was oblivious of the outside world until, faintly at first, but unmistakably in the clear air there came the whiff of tobacco.

Glancing over to the other bank Archie saw, seated on a boulder, the grey figure of a man. He sat perfectly still, his eyes glued to the point of interest, puffing gravely at his pipe.

In a moment Archie's whole world crashed about him. The silent figure was his arch-enemy, Mr Rory McGilp, the estate headkeeper himself whom, Archie had been assured, was far away on Loch Tulla to visit a sick son.

Now, it is true to say that Archie was his own master, but only in the sense that if he could wrest a living from the barren lands as his father had done before him, he was welcome. The sporting rights, however, including the fishing for salmon, remained in the domain of the laird. This, in the tolerant atmosphere of the day, would not have caused Archie much unease were it not that the new laird, a 'foreigner from the south', had recently purchased the property and was strict about enforcing his rights. Already Archie had been marched into the factor's office no less than three times. On the last occasion he had been given the final ultimatum: one more time and he would be out of his little cottage in Glen Nant, lock, stock and baggage.

Even if now he were to cut and run (perish the thought), it would do him no good. He had been caught fair and square.

Unable to bear the silence any longer, Archie cried out to the man on the other shore, 'It's a fine day this!'

'It'll be a day you'll be wishing it was night, before I've done wi' ye!' was the grim answer that came back, and Archie almost fell into the river at the response.

'It'll be a bad day's work for me this!' he cried out almost in a whine.

'It'll be all that, my man!' replied the keeper grimly.

Just then Archie caught his first glimpse of the fish. The salmon almost ran aground in the shallows on the keeper's side and the latter saw the great white belly flash under the thin water. Then the mighty rudder of a tail twisted it round as on a pivot. Something like five feet of blue-brown back came shooting up the pool close to the bank, and then disappeared, like a ghost, in the deep stream above. Archie thought he had hold of a prize, but the other knew it, and his experienced eye told him that he had just seen the heaviest salmon which had ever come into his ken either in or out of the Awe. 'By God, he *is* a fish!' he cried to himself, as with straining eyes he followed its wake in the water.

Great, indeed, was this keeper's wrath and indignation. It was bad enough that this poaching crofter should be at the river at all, but that he should fall on such a piece of luck as this was almost more than mortal man could bear. It made matters still worse for him to think that he had been sitting for half an hour within twenty yards of the fish, and might have been playing him himself—if only he had known.

If Rory McGilp was miserable, imagine Archie's plight. He was more the captive of the great fish, than the fish was his. If ever he needed the help of a sympathetic friend, now was the time.

The fish moved down to the tail of the pool, and sunk himself there. He got his nose upstream, and began to 'jig' at the line, each jig taking him a little further down, and each vibration communicating a dreadful shock to the heart of the man above. 'In five minutes,' thought Archie, 'I'll be likely a mile down, with my rod broken, and that old heathen grinning at me.' Oh, for a friend now!

'Rory!' he cried out softly to his enemy—'Rory!' But no answer came back across the water. Rory sat like a carved statue on his rock.

'Mr McGilp!—my fingers is cut to the quick! Will ye no pitch a stone in below him and turn him up?' Still there was no answer. 'My back's fairly broken!' cried Archie piteously.

'I'm right glad to hear it!' roared back the keeper.

'He's forty pounds weight!' cried Archie appealingly.

'HE'S SIXTY!' screamed Rory, jumping off his rock, and dancing about on the bank. 'You poaching deevil! I hope he'll break your neck and drown you afterwards!'

'Oh—what'll I do if he goes down?' howled the other man, 'he's off—he's off—what'll I do if he goes down?'

The fish lay now on the top of the rapid stream right on the lip of the pool, furiously flapping his tail.

'Give him line!' shouted Rory, 'you great fule!'

Archie lowered the point of his rod, and the fish—as they so often will—stopped at the strain being taken off, but he was too far down to get back. Foot by foot he walloped down; he was fairly out of the pool, he got into the stream, he struggled against it for a moment, and the next he was raging away down the river; now deep down in it, now showing his huge breadth of tail at the top, turning over and over like a porpoise, careless where he went so long as he got clear.

Archie stood in the old place on the bank with his mouth open and most of his hundred yards of line run out, as incapable of checking its movement as if it had been a hundredweight of iron.

'Rin! rin! after him!' roared Rory, forgetting himself again. 'Keep him in. No, let him alone,' was his second thought 'let him be! he'll never get by the point!'

The keeper ran down the bank, hopping lightly over the boulders, and never taking his eye off the bit of foaming water where he judged the runaway to be; and Archie, his first stupefaction over, did the same, and got a slight pull on the salmon some two hundred yards further down.

Rory, when coming up in the morning, had left his rod here, and now got possession of it, and of his gaff, which latter he slung over his back.

To Archie, it seemed as if the end had come, and he would be able to reel up—what he had left—and go home to make arrangements for his 'flitting'. The fish made a wild rush up the river, turned above a big upstanding stone, and then swam slowly down again. The line touched the stone, and Archie could not clear it; the surface was smooth, and it still ran a little, but the end was near: unless the salmon at once retraced his path, he was a free salmon soon.

A good spring landed Rory out on a green-topped slippery boulder with twelve inches of water running over it. He heard the reel opposite give out line in sudden uncertain jerks; he caught sight of a huge bar of yellowish-white coming wobbling down towards him—lost it—saw it again, and delivered his stroke. Up came the great wriggling, curling mass—bright silver now—out of the river; with both hands close to the gaff-head, he half lifted half dragged the fish to shore, struggling, and all but losing his footing in the passage; then up the bank with it till he was able to lie down on it and get his hand into its gills.

Twenty minutes later Archie, with a sinking heart, had crossed the bridge of Awe and travelled up the north bank. The keeper was sitting on a stone, quietly smoking, with no trace of anger on his face, and before him, on a bit of smooth thymey turf, lay a salmon such as many a man has dreamt about, but few, indeed, seen with mortal eyes. Then for the first time that day the poor crofter forgot his troubles: for half a minute his only feel was one of intense pride—at such a victory.

'Well—he's safe now,' Rory said at length.

'Ay!' replied Archie, still gaping at him.

'Erchibald,' went on the keeper, 'Oh, man! you worked him just deevilsih!' The other shook his head deprecatingly. 'Just deevilsih!—frae start tae finish!'

'That was no' a bad bit o' work for a man o' my years,' the keeper continued. 'Gin I hadna been waiting for him there when he came by, it's little you'd have ever seen of your fish!'

'I ken that fine,' said Archie.

'Gin I had no' been quick enough to slip it into him there—it would be at Bonawe he would be by this time.'

'I'm believing that,' replied the crofter.

'It was no' an easy job neither. Stand you on yon stane and see what footing you'll have.'

'There was few could do it, indeed, Mr McGilp.'

'He was far more like a stirk to lift out of the water than a decent saumon!'

'He was, Mr McGilp—far more, indeed, like a very heavy stirk!'

'If it hadna been my knowledge of all they sunken rocks, and shouting myself hoarse to guide you, where would you have been, my man, by this time?'

'It was your inteemate acquaintance with the stanes which saved me, indeed,' once more agreed the crofter.

'There's no anither man in the whole wide world could have steered you down yon places as I did!'

'There is certainly not one in many hundred score would have taken such a vast o' trouble about it.'

'I gaffed him—an' I told you the road to take him—an' saved him many a time. . . .'

'You did all that an' more, Mr McGilp. It's much obligeed. . . .'

'Doubt I made the varra fly that rose him?'

'You did that, indeed,' said poor Archie, hopelessly. (He had made it himself the night before.)

'Dod!' cried the keeper, 'I believe I got yon muckel fish myself!!'

The other stared at him.

'Erchie, lad,' said the keeper—and the voice of the man was changed now, and he spoke so softly and low it was difficult to recognise the same organ which a few minutes before had been hurling denunciations across the river—'I've been fishing here all my life; man and boy I've been fishing here for nearly fifty years, an' I never yet had the luck to get the grip of such a fish as that!'

MacCorquodale looked at him curiously, and he was never able to say positively—he was never quite sure in his own mind—whether it was a tear which rolled down over the rough cheek or not. Then there was a long silence.

'An' where will it be ye'll be flitting to?' the old man asked, in quite another tone, and so suddenly that it made the crofter—deep in reverie—jump.

'Where'll I be—where—off!—Mr McGilp!'

'I believe I got yon muckel fish MYSELL!' with great emphasis on the last word.

Archie looked north and east and west, and then at the salmon.

'MYSELL' as if finally and for the last time.

'I believe—that—too,' said Archie, with a groan. The last three words came out with a gulp.

'Well—he'll be an ugly burden to bearaway doun. But a man canna pick an' choose as he would in this world! Good day to you then, Erchibald. And you might be going on wi' that new bit o' garden you're sae proud of; I'll gie you a wheen grand potatoes—next year—for seed for't.'

It is difficult to know whether to feel sad or glad for Archie. One can only hope, at least, that he got his sack of seed potatoes!

It is certainly true, however, that there are few poachers today after the mould of Archie; those for whom the thrill of catching a fish fairly by rod and line is at least as great if not a greater incentive than procuring a welcome addition to a frugal table.

Many and various are the methods of the present day poacher. The more traditional still practise a modified version of burning the

Until the mid-nineteenth century the salmon runs were widely regarded as a seasonal bonanza. Huge numbers of fish were netted and speared from the rivers, often on the spawning beds.

water by use of a strong light and a long handled gaff in low water. The gaff, incidentally, being known euphemistically amongst the fraternity as The Blacksmith's Fly. Others, more destructively, use a net, fished in the same way as the licensed estuary netters by which the salmon are encircled and pulled ashore, trapped in the bag of the net.

I was, on one occasion, involved in an operation of this sort, if not entirely legally, at least with some measure of moral justification.

I had a friend who owned a splendid stretch on a river which it would be foolhardy to name. It was his habit to let the top half of his water to a tenant with whom he had a gentleman's agreement whereby if the salmon running up were on his beat he would invite his tenant down to fish. Equally, if they passed through to the upper beat the compliment would be exchanged.

It so happened, that his tenant of many years died and he was forced to find a new one. The same arrangement was arrived at and the new tenant happily availed himself of the invitation to fish the low water. Then there came a splash of rain and the fish moved on to a fine holding pool on the tenant's water. Not only was the telephoned invitation not forthcoming, but my friend's ghillie was informed that neither the laird nor any of his guests would be welcome.

It was under these circumstances that revenge was plotted. Ably assisted by his own ghillie and with a 'blind eye' agreement with the water baliff (who let it be known where a confiscated net could be found) the deed was done—and great fun it proved to be.

Next morning, when the tenant arrived on the water, which the day before had been asplash with fish, not a fin moved. They were, in fact, not in the Laird's larder, but back where they started from, the better part of a mile downstream; no doubt wondering about the curious ways of men.

There is no doubt, however, that netting on a river can exact a heavy toll, but on a well-keepered water it is not an easy operation to carry out undetected.

There are however methods infinitely more deadly and destructive which are becoming ever more common.

A long roll of wire netting, for example, can be extended diagonally across the entire width of a river in those long stretches of shallow water between wooded banks. The running salmon encounter the wire and move along it until they reach the upstream end beneath the bank. Every evening or morning the poacher visits his barrier with a long gaff and finds the fish ready and waiting. He

A novel method of taking salmon practised by the French and Spaniards.

extracts several before they scatter, puts them in his sack and disappears. Like the poacher, the salmon will be back there the next day.

Weighted trebles used with a rod or hand-line for 'snatching' can be particularly effective in low water. A stick of dynamite thrown into a 'holding' pool results in a crowd of stunned fish which can easily be netted or gaffed out at its tail. A churn of milk poured into a small pool in low water will, effectively, asphyxiate every fish there.

The deadliest method of all is the use of Cymag. This, without adornment, is cyanide. It kills not only the full-grown salmon, but the parr, the trout, the minnows, the caddis larvae, the freshwater shrimps and so on down to the smallest water-mite. It kills them not by poisoning, but by removing the oxygen from the water. The fish leap into the air and thrash on the surface, returning again and again to the polluted water until, quite simply, nothing moves. It is the most dreadful form of poaching ever devised—indiscriminate slaughter on a grand scale.

Today the price of salmon is very high indeed. Even the small—time poacher can expect a very substantial return for his efforts. A good night's work might earn him upwards of two hundred pounds.

It is natural that this sort of money should attract big-time operators. Moreover the big-time operator has other advantages not enjoyed in a less scientifically developed age.

Formerly salmon had to be disposed of quickly. Now with the advent of the deep freeze this is no longer a consideration. At the same time vastly improved road and rail services have brought the lucrative London and Continental markets within easy reach.

The latest weapon in the poachers' armoury is easily the most deadly—it is the monofil net used along the coast. It enables the poaching gangs to capture very large quantities of fish indeed and no longer confines the poachers' activities to the river bank.

The monofil net, unlike the traditional drift nets used by trawlermen, is virtually invisible in the water. It is also extremely light so that lengths of up to a thousand yards or more can be readily transported and easily stowed away on a boat.

Thus the salmon already facing a new danger in the activities of the deep-sea netter has yet another hazard to overcome before it reaches the relative safety of its home river.

The migrating salmon whilst at sea travel in large shoals within ten feet of the surface. With their strongly developed sense of self-preservation they would, under no circumstances, swim into a visible net, but the monofil net is lethal.

Perhaps what is happening on the Grimersta river in North

Anonymous figures in the dawn.

Lewis, one of our finest salmon rivers, is a good illustration of the seriousness of the organised gangs.

The Grimersta is a short stretch of river only six miles long, but it gives access to a network of inland lochs. To look at a map of western Lewis is to realise that it consists almost as much of water as of land.

The run of salmon is remarkable and the fishing renowned. The best stretch of fishing is owned by a syndicate of wealthy sportsmen none of whom live on the island all the year round.

Since time immemorial, the poaching of salmon has been part of the way of life of the island with absentee landlords being regarded as particularly fair game.

When the late Mrs Elizabeth Perrins owned and lived on the Garrynahine Estate, which also has a stretch of the Grimersta, the fact that she was an extremely popular figure who did a great deal for the island did not exempt her from the attentions of the poachers, but there was little rancour on either side. If she were alive today she would find the spirit of days past to have completely evaporated. Where traditionally the local crofters went out on their own or in pairs, now the poachers are largely gangs of youths from populated centres like Stornoway on the other side of the island. In many cases they are armed and quite ruthless in their pursuit of easy money.

A typical incident, which is related with wry humour by a peer of the realm, who is a prominent member of the Grimersta Syndicate, is as follows:

He was fishing by himself around dusk when he saw a figure behind him on a bank silhouetted against the sky. 'Who are you?' His Lordship enquired, knowing only too well.

'. . .off' came the reply and immediately five or six other heads rose out of the heather.

What did His Lordship do?

'I . . . ed off, of course' he shrugs with resignation.

Last season the situation got so bad that the Syndicate hired a patrol boat at very considerable expense with a crew of six determined men. They managed to cut quite a few nets, but on occasions they found themselves looking down the wrong end of a gun, although clubs were more usually carried by the gangs.

The hiring of this patrol boat came under heavy criticism as evidence of the callous disregard by 'foreigners' of what the islanders regard as their undisputed rights.

So strong was this feeling that a frogman, equipped with a brace and bit, swam out to the patrol boat at night and attempted to hole her below the water line. He was captured and prosecuted but it made him a local hero.

In fact, it is quite impossible to hire ghillies and watchers on the island as no islander will undertake the work not only because it is more profitable to poach, but it would also result in making him a social pariah.

Some of the poachers admit that this large scale poaching, coupled with the deep sea netting in the Atlantic, will inevitably result in their eventually being no salmon. Their attitude is that this is regrettable but not a compelling enough reason for them to at least attempt to limit their depredations.

In 1862 the first major legislation for the protection of the salmon was introduced in the Salmon Fisheries (Scotland) Acts. This was revised in a new Act in 1951. But the whole gist of the Acts is not geared for dealing with poaching as a fully-fledged business. The penalties are aimed at the suppression of that happy breed, the one-for-the-pot poacher.

If this chapter occasionally reads as though it is a poacher's manual, then it is only because it is essential that salmon fishermen are aware of as many different methods of poaching salmon as possible. *And* that they understand the nature of the problem.

As often as not, the skillful amateur with his handline and weighted trebles ends up in court, while the organised gang with their monofil nets or diving gear and their wireless tuned into the local police station escape unhindered.

Who can seriously doubt the need for new legislation?

And if you find the local police sergeant as I have done happily, if rather furtively, fishing your beat. Well . . . you should have offered him a day in the first place.

THE SPORTSMAN ABROAD

'The Sportsman is a Being sui generis*; he is a plant—as it were—of pure English growth. Who ever heard of a Frenchman travelling some twelve or fifteen hundred miles for the avowed purpose of catching salmon?'*

Jones's Guide to Norway, *1848*

The British passion for empire building is also reflected in their passion for taking over almost anything in Europe which, in their view, is too good for mere foreigners.

It was, of course, the British who 'invented' Switzerland and were the first to indulge in the improbable sport of hurtling down a mountainside balanced precariously on two small strips of wood known as skis.

It was the British aristocracy who were the first to discover the delights of the South of France and Biarritz with its Promenade Edward VII and Rue Reine Victoria, its English Club and, until comparatively recent times, its pack of English foxhounds. In Edwardian times, it was more English than England, and made a nice change from Brighton.

So it was in sport. From partridge shooting in Spain to boar hunting in the Ardennes, to pheasant shooting in Hungary they came, and saw and took it over as their birthright and nobody was happier than the French or the Spaniards or the Hungarians or the Swiss.

As keen as any to seek out new playgrounds were the great body of dedicated salmon fishermen.

The fishing pilgrimage to Norway began surprisingly early in the nineteenth century. In 1848 a little guide appeared from the publishing offices of J. Jones at 111 Jermyn Street, edited by Frederic Tolfrey. It is called *Jones's Guide to Norway and Salmon-fisher's Pocket Companion* and contains six chapters on every aspect of Norwegian salmon fishing. The anonymous contributors dealt with the difficulties of travelling, including letters of credit, Norwegian cooking and the amusements in Hamburg on the way. Concerning Hamburg, the unknown writer commented 'Of the morality of the *soirées dansantes* it comes not within our province to speak.' But whether it was in his province or not (and one imagines it was) he went on enthusiastically, 'Here fun, revelry and mirth are in the ascendant . . . if the fascinating fair ones—bless their rotundities!—do occasionally take a gallop over the marriage course, without the formality of a Priest's licence, the little rogues do it so cleverly and clandestinely that we cannot find it in our hearts to condemn them.'

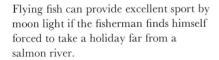

Flying fish can provide excellent sport by moon light if the fisherman finds himself forced to take a holiday far from a salmon river.

It was largely the English grandees who pioneered Norway as a salmon fisherman's paradise. They would arrive in their yachts with their retinues, take over complete hotels and fish the salmon-rich rivers like the Aaro or the Sundal with an enthusiasm and dedication which both surprised and delighted the Norwegians.

In the wake of real rich like the Dukes of Westminster and Sutherland, the Marquis of Londonderry and others in the top echelon of society, there followed the dedicated enthusiast for whom the catching of fish was more important than the socialising.

There is no doubt that the salmon fishing in Norway was, and is, of superb quality although it is noticeable that the open-handed welcome of the pioneering years is now more cautious and the commercial consideration of greater importance. But, where else on the fishermen's horizons is this not true?

Salmon fishermen of all breeds of sportsmen seem the most ready to record their exploits in print.

Much has been written about fishing in Norway at the turn of the century. This report by Thomas Stanford, published by Longman Green in 1902, is as typical as any.

Fishing at Lervick he records:

It is strange how occasionally fish will have the fly, regardless of their brethren having been hooked and escaped, or been hooked and killed, before their eyes. On a June night in the great fishing season of 1900, I stood beside C., as he fished from The Bank, and for a time a fish rose every cast he made. Some merely gave a 'pull', others were hooked and lost, others were played and killed; but still as the fly came round a fish came at it. It was at 4 am and the sun was coming over the hill, and the ebb-tide had fallen almost to low water. The fish were lying in only three or four feet of water, and for some unknown

A hardy Victorian showing Olaf that the British are made of sterner stuff.

reason were madly on the take. C. was dropping from fatigue, and could hardly hold his rod up to play the last, an 18-pounder, which ran wildly for the Fos. But such occasions, to be marked with a white stone, are few and far between.

In the long run, our best sport has been had at night. Major Traherne's theory that fish do not take well in the small hours of the morning does not hold good here. But fish will frequently take in the daytime, especially before noon, and in the brightest sun. A small Silver Grey or Silver Doctor is then the most killing fly. Our record fish was killed on a Silver Grey on a bright day, about noon. On a dark day we have found the Jock Scot invincible. The worst time undoubtedly is late in the afternoon, when the sun is shining directly up the river, but I have known fish take even then.

The angler's ambition is ever to kill a really big fish, but it is not always the biggest fish that fight most pluckily for their lives. I met with an instance of this a few years ago when fishing the Sundal River. It was clearing after a spate; the previous day it had been too big and too dirty for sport. By the side of a strong running stream I hooked a fish, but until he was on the shore I had no suspicion of his size. He was extremely sluggish, and seemed averse to going out into the stream, and never, I think, took out five yards of line. Within six minutes of my hooking him he drifted close to the bank, when my gillie put the gaff into him and dragged him ashore. Then we saw to our surprise and delight that he was a great fat cock fish; and they were increased when we found that he actually scaled 42 lb. I was fishing with single gut and a medium sized Jock Scot, and with the river as it was the odds were on the fish, if he had only played the game. It is possible that he had been travelling and was tired. I have met with similar instances of dull fish in our upper waters here; but in the tidal water we are not troubled with such sluggards, and I do not remember to have killed a fish in it which did not make a creditable fight.

Our anticipations of a good year, based on the big river and the great reserve of snow, seem, as June is passing away, hardly likely to be realised. The conditions are quite abnormal. The river is unusually high, and the water unusually cold. Fish run into Lervik and Ladder Pools, but they do not seem to lie there. Nor do I think that they frequent the great holes under the Fos, and there is no run of fish up the ladder. Some are lying in the Lower Stream, and others I believe return with the ebb-tide to the fjord, whence they will doubtless run up again when the conditions alter. There do not seem to be many fish, certainly far fewer are to be seen jumping than usual. At such times sport is uncertain and the element of luck plays a great part. In normal times one rod will probably have very much the same sport as the other, but when fish are few or coy, it is all a matter of fortune. So it was one day soon after our arrival. We began at 8 am on the ebb-tide. C., usually a most successful angler, tried an 'Eagle' in the still water from the Lower Bank. It was an old fly, and the gut loop must have been rotten, for as a fish took it, it broke. Fortune does not readily forgive such a waste of opportunity and not another rise did poor C get the whole day. For me, it was a day of days. On the morning ebb I killed three fish in Lervik, 13, 12 and 22 lb; on the afternoon flood, wading from the Lower Bank, three, of 15, 13 and 12 lb, and when I went out again to fish Lervik on the evening ebb, by all the rules the best chance of the twenty-four hours, it looked as though I might break all records. But it was not to be. Lervik was drawn blank, and I was beginning to despair when I got a 16-pounder in a backwater at the head of the Lower Stream, where we very seldom cast a fly. So I had seven fish, weighing 103 lb.

I quote Thomas Stanford at some length not only because it is a good description of fishing a typical Norwegian water, but also shows that the nature of angler does not change. Note the satisfaction that 'Major Treherne's theory that fish do not take well in the morning does not hold good here', 'so sucks to the Major!' one feels he would like to add. Nor can he hide his delight that 'C., usually a most successful angler' has his pretension as a fisherman well and truly shown up. Would he have reported it as a 'day of days' had the position been reversed?!

It would seem that big bags, if by no means a matter of course, were, and for that matter still are, more predictable than can be expected on our home rivers. Certainly a higher proportion of very large fish was the order of the day. Occasionally there were fabulous catches: seven fish from the Aaro in one day weighing 239 lb, 29 fish in one night from the Alten weighing 600 lb. And then the astonishing total of 1,352 salmon and grilse in $51\frac{1}{2}$ days to two rods fishing the fly in South Norway in 1924.

There is some indication, however, that the really big Norwegian fish are now much rarer than formerly. Charles Ritz, an enthusiastic fisherman of worldwide repute, fishing the Aaro after the war, writes graphically of titanic struggles. But I can find no record of his catching a fish over 30 lb. On the other hand, as it was his custom to fish with only a $9\frac{1}{2}$ ft. rod and light tackle, in a river as fast-flowing as the Aaro, perhaps many of those who broke him were real tritons.

It is perhaps interesting here to compare the salmon fishing in

Norwegian rivers are famous for their strong currents and precarious
wading. Casting platforms are a common sight on many waters. Here
a pool on the River Aurland is ringed with such platforms.

Norwegian rivers with Canada, which has for long been associated
with first class sport. In the early part of the nineteenth century a
General Sir John Macdonald is reputed to have killed 400 salmon
in a week on the Escoumains River in Quebec, though one
imagines this was not to his own rod. However the General
achieved this bag (and I imagine a net came into it before rather
than after hooking some of the fish) salmon were astonishingly
prolific in both the Quebec and New Brunswick provinces in the
last century.

To get some idea of what it is like to fish for salmon which are
literally packed into the river, it is necessary today to go to Alaska
for the Pacific Salmon. There, although the prodigious runs of
salmon have long been known, it is only comparatively recently

that the high degree of organisation necessary to make them accessible to the short-term visitor has become available.

I am indebted to the Marquess Conyngham who made the trip in July 1981 for an interesting account of his experiences.

Our party went for the first week in July, flying from Heathrow to Anchorage, where we spent one night in the Captain Hook Hotel, did some last-minute shopping in a quite amazing sporting store and then took a 45-minute flight by Wien Airliner to Iliamna where we were met by Range Rover and driven to the Lodge at the head of Iliamna Lake which is run by Mr and Mrs Ted Gerbin. The Lodge was comfortable and the food excellent but we had to bring our own booze though on occasions some blueberry wine (home brewed) was provided. Three light aircraft equipped with floats were available to fly us to different fishing grounds. There is so much water that one can land almost anywhere and flying over such wonderful country is quite fascinating.

After an enormous breakfast at 7 am we would divide into parties of three plus guide and pilot and set off.

Without any doubt the highlight for me was the wild Rainbow Trout fishing and I quickly abandoned sunk fly for the dry fly which they will take with enthusiasm. There is often a good catch from about 10 am and, provided one does not cast a shadow or expose oneself, as the water is gin clear, the fish are not too difficult to catch. All fish are released, though if you wanted to have a specimen 6 lbs or over could be kept for mounting and you could keep enough to eat for lunch. To facilitate a quick and easy release we pinched in the barbs and did not seem to lose too many fish.

There were two methods employed on a day's Rainbow

fishing. You either landed well upstream with an inflatable rubber raft and drifted down fishing as you went or proceeded at best speed upstream in a water jet outboard with very shallow draught. Many different fly patterns were successful from Black Gnats to large Sedges and I found a large Tups particularly effective. For the wet fly almost anything, often large and flashy. The weight ranged from $1\frac{1}{2}$ to 8 lbs at this time of year, later in September very heavy Rainbow up to 20 lbs follow the spawning salmon to the headwaters where they feed on shed eggs.

We also fished for Arctic Char and Grayling, the latter more sophisticated than the Rainbow and quite amazing.

The salmon fishing in our case was a very interesting experience though not entirely to my taste. The run reaches its peak of 35,000 Sockeye per hour passing any given point and they do not stop until they reach the spawning grounds by which time they are bright red and ugly.

You position yourself on the river probably 10–15 yards from your neighbour and with Polaroid glasses can plainly see the salmon in an endless chain like ants swimming at a fast walking speed at a depth of 5 or 6 ft. The fly must be got right down to them with quick sinking line and even leaded flies and they are seldom more than 15 yards from the bank. They take sporadically, fight very well and when clean are very beautiful and excellent to eat, but I soon got bored with it.

The Sockeye are, of course, a rather different proposition to our European *Salmo Salar* in that, on their return to the spawning beds, they procreate and die. None attempts the return journey.

Their willingness to take a fly and their indifference to misfortune, however, is interesting when read in conjunction with

Thomas Stanford's report on migratory salmon in Norway quoted earlier.

It is easy to understand 'Mount' Conyngham's growing indifference if almost every cast produces some sort of reaction. Fishing would have few charms if it were always so. Perhaps frustration is the best part!

To the obvious question of how much it costs to indulge in an 'Alaskan Adventure' the answer is door to door and back again £1,600 a week, although obviously on longer stays it would not be proportionately higher.

The question of cost is, of course, an important one although it may have no place when discussing the rival merits of the quality of the sport provided. It may be mentioned in this context that to take a week on a prime stretch of a home river might well show little change from £1,000 if all expenses are taken into consideration.

To return to the problem of catching fish when the odds are against the fisherman, it is worth noting a branch of Canadian fishing which, though it has never been practised with success in this country, is widely used across the Atlantic. This is the technique of dry-fly fishing for salmon. Incidentally, I am glad to be able to report that it was first used *intentionally* for salmon on that true home of the dry fly the Test in Hampshire, where Major J. R. Fraser used it with some, though limited, success in 1906.

The true pioneers of dry-fly fishing for salmon were George La Branche, Edward Ringwood Hewitt and Ambrose Monell. This trio fished mainly on the New Brunswick rivers and particularly the Upsalquitch and the Restigouche. Once both fine salmon rivers, unfortunately they were severely affected by DDT spraying carried out by the forestry authorities in the 1950s, from which they have not completely recovered.

Both La Branche and Hewitt wrote books on their experiences.

Since La Branche's is the one that is best known, and since he also tends to be credited more frequently with developing dry-fly fishing for salmon than Hewitt, it seems only right to quote from Hewitt's *Secrets of the Salmon* (1922) in order to redress the balance. Alas, poor Ambrose Monell does not seem to have written a book at all.

In introducing his experiments in dry-fly fishing, Hewitt wrote:

> When one sees a number of salmon side by side as they often lie in the tail of a pool and watches a regular salmon-fly pass over them or past their very noses without any attention or motion on their part, except to move away if the fly or leader comes too close, one is tempted to wonder if these fish will really take a fly at all under these conditions. And yet it is these very fish at this time which will furnish the best of sport. For some reason they are in a state of mind where the wet fly does not attract them at all. Perhaps they have reverted to the mental state of parr, taking insects off the surface. Let a real fly or a small butterfly float over them and see how often one will rise and suck it in.

Personally, I have never seen a salmon rise to anything *in particular* and certainly never to a butterfly! Just the same, Hewitt tested his theory and discovered that by perfecting a way of presenting the fly to the salmon with a curved cast so that the fly floated down directly over the fish, he got results.

Although Hewitt does not record spectacular numbers of fish the point is that he caught fish in bright, low-water conditions when fishermen using traditional methods as often as not had a blank day.

The tackle he used was extraordinarily light—gut of .010 in.

diameter with a breaking-strain of 3–$3\frac{1}{2}$ lb and a rod that was light even by American standards of the day.

Hewitt, with La Branche and Monell, fished the East coast rivers of Canada in their heyday and also fished extensively in Newfoundland. He himself never came to England after perfecting the dry-fly technique, but La Branche did.

La Branche stayed with the late A. H. E. Wood at Glassel on the Dee, himself a great experimenter in salmon fishing techniques and the pioneer of the greased line. Sadly the dry fly did not have the same success as on his home waters and he caught very few fish in his long stay.

Possibly this was because the temperature of the water, on which great emphasis was laid by Hewitt (60° Farenheit minimum) was wrong, but more probably because of the completely different nature of Scottish and Canadian waters.

Here is an account of one of Edward Hewitt's more successful days on the Restigouche river in July 1921.

On the way as we were passing the great bunch of fish in the springwater I asked if I could break off a hook and show him how they could be made to rise, so that he could catch them later with my type of flies. He told me 'go to it' and hook all I liked. I felt like a convict released from prison. Looking at that bunch just made shivers run up and down my back. I got the canoe in position about sixty feet to the side and placed a nice cast over the edge of the bunch. What I had expected happened, several fish came at once and they almost bumped each other, so none got the fly. The second cast was more successful and a nineteen-pound fish succeeded in beating the others to it. After one jump I handed the rod to Mr B who yelled for me to get another and called to the guide on the

shore to bring Mr A down from the camp at once. By the time
he arrived I was just hooking another fourteen-pound fish and
Mr A got up to the boat just in time to take the rod and go off
down the pool with the fish. Their two sons were in another
boat just behind, so I took another rod and hooked one for
them. It was a great disappointment that the smaller fish were
always quicker than the larger ones, and as they composed the
larger number, they always got the fly first. We only hooked a
few fish of twenty pounds; most of them were fifteen, sixteen,
eighteen pounds. But this is good fishing on light rods. We had
three rods going all the time, and as one salmon was landed the
rod was loaded with another fish in a few minutes. I lost all
count, but the guides said I had fifty-four rises and hooked
fourteen fish, of which they landed eleven. As this is about the
usual proportion of rises to fish hooked, unless the angler is
very lucky and skilful, I think it is probably a correct
estimate. We finally stopped after two hours' fishing with
eleven fish on the bank; more than the four rods had taken
during the past week. Mr B remarked to Mr A: 'You've been
a damn fool and that is bad enough, but to be a damn fool for
thirty years is the limit'.

Who can imagine such excitement on any of our home rivers? But a
word of warning to any rash enthusiast who imagines that this
method is the answer to drought-stricken Scottish spate rivers. The
Canadian rivers are clear and relatively smooth-flowing, the fish
can be easily approached by wading or by canoe and, most
importantly, there are an awful lot of fish. Dry-fly fishing for
salmon is a specialised technique, for the line must be cast so that it
lands with a curve at the end and great skill is required when
tightening on a rising fish. Do not think that putting a large Soldier

Palmer on the end of your standard floating line and casting it over cold peaty water will have a startling effect on the fish. It will merely bore them.

No mention has so far been made of an alarming hazard that confronts all salmon fishermen, but particularly those in Norway, Canada and Iceland. Namely, the bloodthirsty attacks of flies, midges and mosquitoes.

This is not, by the way, a trivial matter. The Blue-Winged Olive and the Mayfly are of interest to the trout fisherman, as are the Yellow Sally and the Pale Watery Dun and a host of others. They have soft, melodic names well suited to their gentle characters. Not so the midge and the horse fly, the fisherman instead is of interest to them.

For these intruders there are a number of offensive sprays, creams and lotions, all of which claim to be absolutely infallible. Needless to say, they are not. Occasionally, they will repel recconnoitring patrols, but in my experience they are hopeless in the face of a frontal assault by a full-blown division. Unless, of course, you adopt the tactics of one fisherman I know. This requires a particularly bloody lump of pig's, lamb's or calf's liver and an old hat. The liver is tied securely to the top of the hat, the hat is placed securely on top of the fisherman's head, and the midges, horse flies and sundry horrors are able to dine undisturbed on the top floor. Like all good arrangements, it is one that suits everybody.

In Norway, Canada and Iceland, however, there is a creature that makes the midge and the horse fly seem vegetarian in their habits. This is the black fly, which like the flies in the Third Plague of Egypt, occurs in 'grievous swarms'. Fortunately, they only hatch for short periods of a fortnight or so during the summer, but when they are about they are diabolical.

There is only one successful solution that I have ever heard of

for the black fly. It comes from an early account of fishing in
Canada:

I extracted from my box another fiery brown and proceeded
to attach it to my casting line, when I found myself gasping for
breath and nearly blinded with smoke. On turning round I
perceived one fire of dead leaves, and withered branches, and
wet drift wood, and damp grass, giving out volumes of smoke,
on my right hand, another on my left, and my amiable Indian
busily employed in kindling a third immediately and closely
behind me. The day was bright, the sun was intensely hot, and
the rock on which we stood was exposed to all his rays; so that
what could be his object in increasing the already ardent heat
was a mystery to me, until having interrogated to him as well
as I could by pantomime, he pointed to the myriads of black
flies which were crawling upon the rock at my feet, and which
he assured me by his signs would long before have fixed their
fangs and left their poison in my forehead and my throat and
behind my ears, were it not for the smoke proceeding from the
fires which he had lighted.

It is Iceland that has perhaps the worst reputation for
carnivorous flies. J. G. Millais, the son of the Pre-Raphaelite
painter John Everett Millais, mentions seeing a black pony in
Iceland near Lake Myvatn which suddenly turned piebald upon
his approach as the black flies rose in a cloud above it. Myvatn,
appropriately enough is the Icelandic for 'midge'. Happily,
Iceland's reputation as a piscatorial El Dorado overshadows the
fame of its flies.

Icelandic salmon fishing is highly valued (and literally, for it is
extremely expensive nowadays) for two reasons. Firstly, the rivers

are by and large fast-flowing and clear so that they are a joy to fish with the fly. And secondly, although the average weight of the salmon is relatively small (under 10 lb), and there are no monsters such as are found in Norway, they are there in profusion. John Ashley Cooper, who has fished in Iceland extensively and who rented a river there for a number of years, has stories of huge bags of grilse on the West Coast rivers, running on rare occasions to fifty or sixty fish to a single rod in a day.

Like so many other remote rivers, Icelandic waters can be reached today by helicopter and light aircraft with considerable ease. This seems a pity. One of the charms that emerges from old reports of fishing expeditions to far-flung corners of the world seems to have been sense of adventure and isolation.

One man who fished widely in Iceland in the days when transport was mainly by pony was Major-General R. N. Stewart. As far as I know, he only wrote one book, *Experiment in Angling and Some Essays*, published by The Northern Chronicle Office in Inverness in 1947. General Stewart was totally convinced that salmon had 'infra-red' sight. In other words, that they saw the world as though through an infra-red lens. Now this may very well be true, but the theory, combined with the book's title might give the impression that the General was a crashing old bore. Fortunately, it is only necessary to dip into the book at random to discover that he was evidently the most entertaining and adventurous of men. His literary style, if a little arcane, has a dry, ironic flavour that is worth savouring at some length. More to the point, it gives an extremely clear idea of what fishing in Iceland was like before the days of dukes and millionaires.

I have chosen a day from my game book that I consider a good day, because I do not wish my guest to have poor sport;

Convenient and efficient but sadly lacking the romance of transport
by pony.

anyway he might be bored if the fishing were bad. I have not chosen a 'Best' day, but one above the average, it being never well to write of failure; anyway I like my books to have a happy ending even if you do not; so you will have to put up with my day, that is if you accompany me at all.

The date is the 6th of July, the weather is fine, warm for the latitude (about 50 degrees F.), wind southerly and light, incidentally a down-stream wind. We are going to the lowest beat, about six miles from our farm house, and to get there we ride ponies. By the way, Iceland ponies want knowing, but more of this anon.

Olaf, our gillie, has been warned that we want the ponies for 9 a.m. and our usual lunch. But I must introduce Olaf. Olaf is an Icelander, he has attained the age of eighteen, has left school, and is spending his summer as a gillie, not for monetary gain but because he wishes to improve his English, he is going to Copenhagen in the autumn to finish his education, he is a very nice lad, kindly character, very musical, and has great interest in his fellow beings. He is not a fisherman or a naturalist, and he is the world's worst gaffer of fish. However, to-day this is not important because he will be able to beach 90% of any fish we catch, and the odd one he cannot gaff we shall do so ourselves. Olaf is very useful, however, he acts as interpreter, he carries anything, and he is very willing to please and to make the day a success. Let me make it quite plain that in no way do we depend on Olaf to tell us where to fish or what to fish with, for the very simple reason that he has no idea of either, but I would not part with him for anything.

Well, to-day we are lucky. I say lucky because Iceland ponies do not like being caught and have no idea of time, but on this occasion they are ready for us by 9.30 a.m. The lunch is ready, too; Olaf has not forgotten the sacks in which we hope to bring back fish, and we are off.

The road follows our river for about three miles, a road made out of crushed lava, undulating and lumpy, but quite fair going, and we average about 6 m.p.h. We then leave the road and have a mile of good grassland where we can have a gallop, then on to some steep scree ground where the going is bad, and for half a mile only a slow walk is possible, after which more good turf, and we are at the top of our beat.

Now we must hobble our ponies, a job we supervise ourselves, Olaf's hobbling being uncertain, and we off-saddle. I must explain this. All Icelandic saddlery is ancient, they do not appear ever to have new saddlery, and most of it is only kept in place and together by short pieces of assorted string. A reserve of string in the pocket is a wise precaution to carry. I suggest imported string, because Icelandic string is comparable to Icelandic saddlery.

The ponies are left hobbled on what looks to us a succulent grazing ground, but it is never succulent to the ponies' mind, and they find a better one much farther away. We can now turn to the day's business. The time is about 10.30 a.m.

Here, I think, I must describe the landscape and river, or at least that portion of it we are going to fish to-day.

Arctic and sub-arctic landscapes have two aspects. In fine sunny weather, with no wind, they are beautiful and benign, but they can change to a bitter malignant ferocity in the space of a few hours, leaving in the mind of the wayfarer a sense that he may have to face a ruthless struggle for life with all nature opposed to him.

'The stark and sullen solitudes that sentinel the Pole' adequately describes the scene in its ruder moments.

I would not necessarily attribute to the Iceland scenery the animosity that this suggests during the time of year that we go there to fish, when beauty on the grand scale is predominant, and the weather soft and smiling; but any country beyond the Northern limit of trees gives an inner feeling that the menace is there if for the moment latent.

The Iceland scene is rugged, the rivers wild, and on a grander scale than Scottish rivers, and the hand of man has never made their banks easier for the angler as it has done in all good fishing waters in this country.

This in some way adds to the feeling that you are fishing almost virgin water and makes anticipation an even keener emotion than it is on the well-worn banks of the rivers at home.

As you come to the river bank no path makes your progress

easy, no bridges span tributary burns, no snags or obstacles removed; it is all just as it was one thousand years ago, the only change being what nature herself decides in the ebb and flow of the winter ice.

I have travelled far in arctic lands, and I have a liking for them; all the men I have met who know them feel as I do.

'It grips you like some kind of sinning,
It twists you from foe to a friend.'

In size it is what I call a medium river which can comfortably be covered by a powerful 11 foot rod and short waders in calm weather. Our water is the lowest beat, where the river flows into the Arctic Ocean. It has flowed from its source through flat ground, rocky ground, gorges, and finally comes out into a plain, at the end of which the estuary begins. The pools are long, fairly deep in places, with good streams at their heads, with still even-flowing flat tails to them. Just below our first pool, called Sika Junction, a large tributary joins the river and helps the volume of water.

The bank we are on is short grass to within fifty yards of the river and then shingle for another 30 or 40 yards; the other side is steeper with a grass bank some 5 to 6 feet in height dropping into deep water. All down this part of the river bits of this bank have broken off and lie in the stream, forming good holding places for fish, furthermore not of such consistency that they will cut the cast should it foul one in playing a fish.

The rest of General Stewart's day's fishing, though entertaining, reads a little as though he was fishing anywhere. Of course, one river is very like another, but the special characteristic of Icelandic rivers is that the upper stretches of many tumble through huge gorges. On such stretches, the fisherman can scramble down to the

Furrows by William Garfit, R.B.A. A steep-sided pool in the upper
reaches of a typical Icelandic river.

water's edge and a companion or ghillie 'direct operations' from
above, being able to see both the fish and the fly. There are also
opportunities for the would-be mountaineer to risk his neck,
though this may not be to everybody's taste. I am indebted to an
enthusiastic friend for permission to reproduce the following
passage from a letter. He says he prefers to remain anonymous, I
imagine because he wishes to save the feelings of his insurers:

At the top of the river a 60 ft waterfall pours off the flat plain
into a gorge. The fall, or foss (the Icelandic word for it), has a

pool to itself which cannot be reached as the cliff runs straight into the river.

The nearest you can approach the foss is a pool called Foss 1. It can only be fished from the left bank, and owing to the cliff, only fished upstream, unless you're prepared to risk climbing the cliff. I did this twice, but as the foss is 3 miles from the nearest track and 10 miles from the nearest farmhouse I normally thought better of it.

Anyway, it's done like this. You scramble up the cliff at the tail of the pool and then work your way out and up along a series of ledges. This is exhilarating in its own right as the spray from the foss blows downstream on to one side of your face, the rod has to be held in one hand and studded waders slip on the rock. You edge along to as near the neck of the pool as possible and then turn round. That sounds easy. It isn't as the ledges are no more than 1 ft across.

Looking down, the main part of the pool is a deep 'pot'. I don't know how deep, I'd guess about 30 ft, though to be honest despite the crystal-clear water you can't see the bottom. Only different bunches of salmon and grilse, a few Arctic char and the odd brown trout.

By this time you feel like a gnat perched over an aquarium. The first essential is to get properly wedged into position. Then, with the sun shining through the spray and making a rainbow further up the gorge beneath the foss, you pick a fish. The fun about this is that they all look double their actual size owing to the refraction of the water.

Casting is, from necessity unorthodox. A sort of sideways flick with a bit of a roll in it. Spey casting would probably work best of all, but I've never learnt how to do it. Anyway, the line straightens out quite well as it falls. You then drag the fly across the nose of your fish, and it either takes or it doesn't. There's no proper fishing the fly. Often they just follow the fly into the side rather languidly.

Then, for no apparent reason, one'll suddenly hurl itself on the fly and make off like a handbag-snatcher. That's when you start to regret the whole enterprise. The fish invariably runs straight across the pool into the current on the other side and then heads off downstream. It pulls one way and you lean the other. After a while it's happily leaping about in the next pool down and the backing's half way out. Obviously time to move. To tell the truth, I've never been quite sure exactly how to get down. The best way seems to be to turn round, trap the rod under one arm and see how it goes. The fish, meanwhile, tears about in the next pool jerking away at the rod and pulling you off-balance every time you try to slide down to the next ledge. Sometimes it seems to be a good idea to turn round again and play it some more in an attempt to subdue it. In fact, its better to ignore the fish entirely until you're back on the shingle.

By the way, the real advantage of catching fish this way, is that you never mind if you lose one . . .

Of course, it by no means essential to travel abroad to find first-class fishing. Although it is not often in our home rivers that the salmon really declare a field day but it does happen from time to time and when it does it matches anything to be experienced on the other side of the Atlantic.

There are few of the really great salmon rivers in this country on which these exceptional days do not occur.

It is often after a lengthy period of drought and low water when the fish are massed in the big pools, sullen and listless. It is then that the fisherman prays for rain. There is no more comforting sound,

54 Salmon and grilse weighing a total of 314 lb. This record catch was made on the lower loch of the Grimersta on the Isle of Lewis by A. M. Naylor on 28 August 1888, between 9.30 a.m. and 6.30 p.m. The party of three rods took 333 fish for the week, a catch made possible by the creation of an artificial spate.

after days of hopeless endeavour on the river, to waken in the night and hear the rain pelting down outside and know that the fresh water will stir the salmon into activity far beyond the hopes of the most greedy of fishermen.

On one beat of the Grimersta a record bag for a spate river of 54 salmon were taken in a single day in 1888. How many were hooked and lost history does not relate. The slower rising rivers like the Tay have been known to produce even bigger catches. On the Islamouth pool, for example, when the fish have been lying

140

indecisively for perhaps weeks, a freshening of the water stirs them to a frenzy of activity which results in phenomenal catches.

Of course occasions like these are small test to the skill of the fisherman. The truly dedicated fisherman will derive infinitely greater pleasure in catching a fish in difficult conditions.

To appreciate the satisfaction of pulling off such a 'tour de force', or to be more blunt enjoy such outrageous luck, I can do no better than to quote the late George Cornwallis-West in his amusing book, long since out of print, *Edwardians Go Fishing*, (1932). Relating his experiences when fishing the Irish Blackwater surely the only rival to, it not the equal of the Shannon, he describes the following incident.

Last year when fishing the Blackwater I saw a big fish jump right in the slack water at the very bottom of the pool. My ghillie told me it was useless to try there as the fish never took, but despite his remonstrances I persisted in doing so. More in chaff than with any conviction of success, I said to him: 'With this cast the prawn will be over him—and you'll see what will happen.' To the amazement of both of us the fish took it. He was twenty-three pounds. My ghillie's comment was: 'Shure, it's yourself, sorr, that has the luck of a fat priest.'

FIRST CATCH YOUR FISH

'From much observation I am quite confident that fresh salmon properly cooked with no lobster or other sauce than the water in which it has been boiled, and eaten without potatoes or other objectionable vegetables, in moderate quantity, is perfectly digestible.'

Dr. W. Jamieson, 1891

No fish is easier to cook, and no fish less often cooked well, than the salmon.

To cook a salmon is as easy as making a cup of tea, but, as in tea-making, you must stick to the rules or the result will be a disaster.

Because the quality of salmon varies so greatly according to the length of time it has been in fresh water, make sure that your salmon is as fresh-run as possible. A fresh-run salmon will be a bright, shining silver. The longer they remain in the river, the darker and blotchier they become, 'tartan beasties', as they are apt to be contemptuously described by Scottish ghillies and, in the opinion of many, fit only to be smoked.

Kelts, of course, are uneatable and it is unlikely, to say the least, that a buyer would be offered one, with the reservation that it is not above the moral conscience of a poacher to offer a well-mended kelt to an inexperienced hotelier. Anyone can spot the frayed and generally disreputable appearance of a far-gone fish, but a fish which is well-mended can only be detected by close inspection of the vent and by maggots in the frayed gills. If still in doubt make a slight incision above the tail, and if the flesh is very red return it to the seller with suitable comments.

There was a case recently of an elderly, retired ghillie who had fallen on evil times. The old reprobate had taken to collecting kelts from the river bank and cutting the best steaks from the middle cut which he hawked from door to door in the respectable suburb of a large town.

One of his friends, meeting him in the street as he was doing his rounds and strongly suspecting what he was at, asked him if he was not ashamed of himself.

'Well,' said the kelt salesman guardedly, 'I did pass the home of one of my regular customers the other day. When I saw all the blinds were drawn I didn't have the heart to sell them another bit.'

Incidentally, Frank Buckland, writing in the middle of the last century, advises his friends not to discard altogether the dead kelts found on the bank, for he says: 'The skins of such fish becoming toughened with age are admirably adapted for tanning. When suitably prepared, their skins will make slippers, gloves, or bindings for books.'

Having caught, bought, or been presented with a decent clean-run fish, preferably between eight and twelve pounds, which most *cognoscenti* regard to be the ideal weight, put Mrs Beeton back on the shelf and proceed as follows.

Fill a large pan, or ideally a fish kettle, with water to which vinegar, a bay leaf, an onion, chopped carrots, fennel, if available, and seasonings are added. Put the gutted fish in whole so that it is covered by the water and bring to the boil. Boil for *three minutes only* and then leave in the water until cold. Remove, skin, place on a dish and garnish with cucumber.

Take no notice of the many experts who advocate cooking for so many minutes to the pound. The three-minute rule should be adhered to whatever the weight of the fish, except perhaps where it is an absolute monster, in which case you would be well advised to cut it into steaks and grill them (for about twenty minutes) or poach them for a slightly shorter time in a white wine *court-bouillon*.

Salmon is an ideal fish for deep freezing. Only make sure that it is completely fresh. Pay great attention, as is not always done, to completely removing the gills which can easily ruin the fish. Remember too that the freezer life of a whole salmon is around six months and rather shorter if cut into steaks.

Smoked salmon also keeps well deep frozen but there are many who prefer to unfreeze a fresh salmon and then send it to the smokers. Most of the best smokers in the country will 'bank' your fish in their own deep freeze and smoke when required.

Be careful only that the smoker knows his business and be careful when buying smoked salmon to see that it is of uniform darkish brown with none of those small white lumps that are indicative of a poor smoking technique.

Basically the lighter a fish is smoked the better it will taste but its keeping qualities obviously depend on how heavily it should be smoked on the principle of the longer the heavier.

The traditional method of using only oak chips for smoking is to my mind incomparably the best. I even know of one smoker who not only oak-chip-smoked but also whisky-soaked, but that is an optional extra!

Perhaps almost as important as having your fish correctly smoked is to have it properly cut.

To carve a fresh salmon is relatively easy. Run the knife down the centre of the back and along the whole length of the fish. Cut downwards from the backbone to the middle of the fish, cut through the centre and remove the piece from the back. Cut the lower half of the fish in the same way. A slice of the thick top part should be accompanied by a thinner part from the belly, where the fat of the fish lies.

Carving a smoked salmon is a far greater art. In no case attempt it unless you are equipped with a long flat-bladed knife, excessively sharp. An old-fashioned steel ham knife is perfect, and keep the knife sharpener by you.

If the smoked salmon has been in the freezer, leave it until it is almost, but *not quite*, defrosted so the flesh is firm. Work slowly and methodically, and carve very thinly in as large slices as you can, working from the tail to the shoulder. Inevitably you will have the odd bosh shot and finish up with quite a lot of bits and pieces. Good! These are ideal for making smoked salmon pâté. For approximately half a pound of bits add:

2 oz butter	4 tablespoons double cream
1 tablespoon olive oil	Pinch of cayenne
2 tablespoons lemon juice	

Cream the butter and oil together, add finely minced salmon and blend thoroughly. Beat in lemon juice, cayenne and cream. Served in ramekins, with hot toast, this will earn you quite a reputation in Cordon Bleu circles.

To return to fresh salmon prepared in the classic manner already described; it requires Hollandaise sauce as much as Rolls required Royce or Mr Fortnum required Mr Mason. Hollandaise has a reputation for being difficult which it does not really deserve.

Hollandaise sauce

2 tablespoons white wine vinegar	Salt and pepper
2 eggs	Lemon juice
4 oz butter	

Reduce the vinegar by half by boiling. Beat the eggs in a fireproof basin that fits over a saucepan (or the top half of a double boiler). With the saucepan full of boiling water and the pan on top, whisk in the butter bit by bit until the mixture starts to set. This does not have to be done at the last minute, as the sauce is quite happy to wait in a warm kitchen. An extra knob of butter at the end prevents a skin forming.

Do not, however, accept that the classic way of cooking and serving salmon is by any means the only way. Recipes for cooking salmon go back into the mists of history. How about

'How to Bake a Joll of Fresh Salmon'
from *The Good Huswife's Jewell*, Thomas Dawson, (1696).
Take ginger and salt, and season it, and certain Currans, and cast them about and under it, and let the paste be fine, and take a little Butter and lay it about in the Paste, and set it in the oven for two houres, and serve it.

Or another seventeenth-century recipe on how to 'Seethe Fresh Salmon'.

Take a little water, and as much Beere and Salte, and put thereto Parsley, Time and Rosemarie, and let these boil togetheare. Then put in your Salmon, and make your broth sharpe with some Vinegar.

Or an alternative to Smoked Salmon

Dilled salmon (for 8 people)

3 lb salmon	1 teaspoon of crushed black
$\frac{2}{3}$ cup of salt	peppercorns
$\frac{1}{2}$ cup of sugar	2 large bunches of fresh dill

Clean and fillet the fish. Mix salt, peppers, and sugar, and put
this in the fish. Put a thick layer of chopped dill on all sides, and
put the fish in a dish which you can weigh down with a board.
Weigh it down with 5 to 6 lb weights and leave it in the fridge for
16 to 24 hours. After that scrape the dill, sugar, pepper, and salt,
and serve as smoked salmon. Serve with the following sauce:

1 teaspoon of mild mustard	1 tablespoon of wine vinegar
5 teaspoons of brown sugar	2 tablespoons of cream
1 tablespoon of olive oil	Pinch of black pepper

Mix well together and serve in sauce boat.

André Simon describes this as *gravlax*, a Swedish 'Gentleman's
Relish', 'much appreciated by Scandinavian gourmets'.

Salmon Coulibiac is to fish as Beef Wellington is to meat; a
complicated but very festive and attractive dish. Make the pastry
the day before out of:

10 oz plain flour	$\frac{1}{2}$ level teaspoon sugar
2 eggs	4 tablespoons of milk
$\frac{1}{2}$ oz yeast	Pinch of salt
2 oz butter	

Cream the sugar and yeast together, beat up the eggs and add
them, heat the milk to lukewarm and add that. Rub the butter
into the flour and salt. Pour in the yeast mixture and knead.
Cover the bowl and let it rise in a warm place for three quarters
of an hour. Then store it in a refrigerator till the next day.

An 8 oz piece of salmon will serve four people, and as well as this
you need:

3 oz patna rice	2 oz butter
2 oz finely chopped	2 tabelspoons breadcrumbs
mushrooms	1 tablespoon chopped parsley
1½ oz onions, finely chopped	1 pudding spoon chopped
Butter for frying	tarragon
2 eggs	Salt and pepper
8 fluid o strong fish stock	A little milk

The salmon needs to be half-cooked before assembly so bake it, wrapped in foil, for about a quarter of an hour. Hard boil the eggs, bring the stock to simmering point and cook the rice in it (it will absorb the stock). Fry the onion and mushroom and mix them with the rice. Cool all these ingredients. Make the pastry into two rectangles, one slightly larger than the other. Paint the edges with milk, and spread the rice mixture over one of the rectangles, flake the salmon over it, then the sliced hard boiled eggs and herbs, dot with butter and make up the 'parcel with the other bit of pastry.'

A buttered baking dish or roasting pan should be used to roast the salmon, and the pastry case should be painted with melted butter and sprinkled with breadcrumbs. After about twenty-five minutes at a number 6/400°F oven the dish will be ready, and should be served with a jug of melted butter.

Anyone who thinks it 'a waste' to use salmon in kedgeree instead of a less aristocratic fish is either a fool or has never tasted it. To my mind, salmon kedgeree is a dish fit for a king, and we must all regret the passing of the country house breakfast, with its steaming chafing dishes of spiced kidneys and kedgeree on the sideboard. Served with a green salad salmon kedgeree makes an elegant and delicious dish for luncheon.

1 lb (approx) cold salmon, flaked	2 hard boiled eggs, chopped up
$\frac{1}{4}$ lb patna rice, boiled and dried	2 oz butter
	Dash of cream
	Salt and pepper

Melt the butter in a pan and add the other ingredients. Make sure it is all heated through well before serving. Some people, respecting the Indian origin of kedgeree, dust the finished dish with cayenne pepper.

Finally we must not neglect any left-overs, must we, as Mrs Beeton constantly reminds us.

Left-over pieces can be flaked and combined with whatever mixture of mayonnaise, gelatine and fresh herbs (not forgetting a little cream and the usual seasonings) you favour in order to make salmon mousse. This should be served with brown bread and butter or hot toast.

Alternatively, salmon makes very good fish cakes, mixed with a bechamel base and coated with beaten egg and seasoned flour.

For a cook with an agile mind, salmon presents many opportunities; perhaps as a stuffing for savoury pancakes, the basis of a hot soufflé, mixed as a relish with cucumbers.

I have heard countless times that in the old days servants in large households insisted on having a clause in their contracts that they should not be required to eat salmon more than three times a week.

Personally I doubt the truth of this as in the old days servants were never in a position to insist on anything.

If it be the truth, however, all I can say is that they were very unimaginative cooks.

THE SALMON, THE LAW
AND THE FUTURE

'Quha sa ever be convict of slauchter of Salmonde in time forbidden be the law, he sall pay fourtie shillings for the unlaw, and at the third time, gif he be convict of sik trespasse, he sall tyne his life, or then bye it.'
Scottish Act of Parliament, 1424

That the salmon is a sadly diminished and, indeed, endangered species is a fact which should be recognised by all fishermen, whether they pursue it for their sport or their livelihood. Of course, every season huge quantities of salmon run up some of the Scottish, Icelandic, Norwegian and Canadian rivers. Any casual witness of this spectacle might be inclined to feel that all is well in the world of the salmon. It is not.

Salmon are fragile. They can be destroyed in a multitude of ways. Historically, pollution and the erection of impassable barriers in the shape of dams and weirs have been the greatest agents of destruction. They led to the virtual extinction of salmon in the Portuguese, Spanish, French, Dutch, German, Danish, and North American rivers and if this particular threat does not appear to be so great as it once was, it is because industry is not a particularly practical proposition in the remote and wilder areas of Europe and Canada where the salmon still flourish.

The Salmon, The Law and The Future

Today, of all freshwater fish the salmon probably enjoys more protection by the law than any other species. Unhappily, the law is now so outmoded that it is often inadequate.

The reason is, of course, that the vulnerable life cycle of the Atlantic Salmon is now beset with a far greater number of enemies than ever before and it is not only the poachers who are responsible for upsetting the ecology.

In spite of the most conscientious efforts of the Hydro Electric Board to ensure that their increasing demands should do the minimum damage to the life cycle of the salmon, some damage is inevitable and occasionally quite substantial.

Problems caused by water abstraction are bound to cause damage to fish life particularly on rivers with a low water flow.

Improved drainage both of agricultural and afforestated land has completely changed the nature of many of our rivers. Where in the normal nature of things natural drainage meant that rivers could hold their water for a longer time the more efficient man-made drainage causes rivers to rise and fall far more, quickly creating spate conditions where none existed before.

This in turn has given rise to considerable problems in bank erosion, causing damage to spawning beds where the salmon are at their most vulnerable.

These are all factors against which it is difficult, if not impossible, to legislate and indeed any efforts to do so might not be in the public interest.

On the other hand there is much that can and must be done to ensure the survival of the salmon. The Salmon Protection Act of 1951 did little to improve upon the old Acts of 1845 and 1868. The Hunter Committee set up in 1962 to review the law recommended many changes which were generally welcomed at the time. To this day, twenty years later, not a single recommendation has been implemented by any Government despite electoral promises. The recommendations included administrative ones, like the creation of Area rather than District Boards, and highly practical ones, like a proper licensing system in Scotland and the restriction of netting to the mouths of river systems.

The non-implementation of the Hunter Report can be partly put down to the normal apathy which sets in once a governmentally appointed committee has made its report, but in the case of the Hunter Committee it is not the only reason for inaction. There is, in fact, a very strong lobby which reacts against any measures which might seem to protect private interests as opposed to what they see as the public right, and public right is generally interpreted as the right to break down the barriers of entrenched privilege.

It is a sensitive area only when it becomes a political battlefield; the fight of the have-nots against the haves, the poor against the rich, the bosses against the workers.

This, of course, is not the issue at all. It is at first sight absurd for many of the more prominent members of the various societies for the preservation of this or that in the various branches of field sports to be the most active participants in what are popularly known as 'blood sports'. It is equally absurd for those who emotionally advocate the abolition of blood sports to be, by and large, the same people who advocate the right of everyone to indulge in them.

Against this background of double thinking let us look at the facts in so far as they apply to our friend Salmo Salar.

As we have seen for countless centuries the salmon has had only to contend with its traditional enemies. Its survival from probably prehistoric times has depended on its ability to adapt. Where the Great Auk, and for that matter the Pterodactyl, persisted in reproducing itself by the laying of one single, vulnerable egg, the salmon, like others of the piscine species, accepts a considerable wastage. To deprive the salmon of its natural enemies would be to upset the whole ecology.

The perfect example of this ecological law are the lemmings who, when faced with a problem of overproduction, due to lack of enemies, seek their own solution.

Of the enemies of the salmon which take their toll from the ova stage, to the return from the sea, to the spawning beds, man has been traditionally the least demanding. The wastage from depredations at sea by its natural enemies like the seal are far greater than the combined efforts of the estuary netting stations and the rod and line fishermen. Eels, mergansers, herons, porpoises and many other natural enemies all take their toll.

There is no doubt that the licensed station fisheries can and do affect salmon stocks adversely. Just how greatly is hard to estimate. In the case of Scotland no figures for individual stations are available, whilst in England they are unreliable. The office of the Inspector of Salmon Fisheries for England and Wales tells me that if they send out a reminder for catch returns the figure goes up by 33 per cent!

In Scotland only overall figures are available which cannot be questioned in individual cases. Until these are available the need for limitation by legislation is impossible to identify.

One thing which is certain is that netting at sea, as opposed to the river mouth, is one of the most destructive factors of all, particularly when combined with other forces such as pollution.

Let us consider briefly the statistics relating to the Tyne in the last century where the complete destruction of its river fishing is generally regarded as being due to industrial pollution.

It would seem at least as likely that the incredible number of nets at sea permitted under English law was rather more to blame.

Stake nets running out from the beach in the estuary of the South Esk.
It is one of the anomalies of Scottish and English law that stake nets
are almost entirely outlawed south of the border, yet in frequent use
on the northern side.

Augustus Grimble, who spent much of his life touring salmon
rivers in the United Kingdom, found the Tyne to be in a sorry state
as far as salmon were concerned in the 1860s. Largely it was

Netting in the Taw Estuary. This form of fishing is arduous and often poorly rewarded. The netsmen only catch fish moving around or running into the estuary. In addition, the passage of a shoal of salmon must coincide with the sweep of the net. Only in long droughts, when fish are trapped in the estuary for long periods, is it detrimental to the stock.

thought due to the Newcastle shipping and sewage. In 1864, the stake nets were outlawed in English waters, though not in Scotland (an absurd anomaly that exists to this day). In 1867, a dam at

Bywell, twenty-three miles upstream, was blown up and the salmon were able to reach their spawning grounds.

Immediately, despite sewage pouring into the river estuary, the fishing returns improved dramatically. The netted fish in 1865 totalled only 5,996. By 1872, a catch of 129,100 was recorded. Hang nets, however, had been introduced off the Northumberland Coast in 1867. These grew unchecked until, by 1891, there were 25 miles of nets to 22 miles of coastline. By the end of the century the salmon catch had fallen to 13,000.

Now the figures, may, like all statistics, be partially inaccurate, but they are not so inaccurate as to make one conclusion inescapable. Able to reach their spawning grounds again, the salmon managed to overcome all hazards until the huge increase in the number of nets, and not merely pollution, finally destroyed them. Today, the Tyne Fisheries net around 90,000 fish a year, but of these more than 94 per cent are salmon headed for Scottish waters further north. Much to the fury of the Scots. The rod catch, which reached 3,000 in Grimble's day is now only just above single figures.

With advances in modern technology, notably radar, the migrations of the salmon can be accurately plotted. It is unfortunate that at the same time improved fishing technniques enable deep-sea fishing fleets to capture them.

Despite the most vigorous representation within the European Community (for which the Atlantic Salmon Trust must take much credit) to make the taking of migratory salmon at sea illegal, literally thousands of *tons* of salmon are taken annually. Currently the Faroese, who are outside the European Community, are legally taking salmon in very large numbers and despite the co-operation of other countries concerned with the preservation of salmon stocks such as Norway and Iceland, illegal fishing is still carried on by boats of other nationalities without a great deal of interference.

It is a matter of general agreement that to continue taking such a vast number of migratory salmon is certain to result in the rapid decline of stocks and ultimately the virtual annihilation of the salmon as a wild fish. The situation with regard to home waters has changed considerably since the 'good old days' when it was a matter of the local poacher against authority. The factors which have brought about this change are not far to seek. The most basic one is economics. Before the war the price of salmon was low. Even fish legitimately caught and sold to reputable dealers fetched only a few shillings a pound. Illegally caught salmon fetched even less so that for the most part the poacher's main motivation was not financial gain and certainly not the pursuit of fortune.

Now the financial picture is quite different. Fast carriage makes the lucrative markets in the South available. The advent of the deep freeze makes the storing of fish in the event of a temporary slump in the market, practical. To point to the causes is easy enough, but to suggest a solution is harder. There are, however, one or two areas where tighter legislation would appear obvious.

Certainly the anomalies as they exist between English and Scottish law should be standardised and in particular with regard to the abolition of sea netting.

When the game laws were introduced to counteract the vast rise in poaching of game following the invention of the shot gun one of the most effective pieces of legislation was to ban the sale of game to anyone other than a *licensed* game dealer and the dealer has the obligation to ensure that the game he buys is legitimately come by.

It is perhaps not generally known that once a salmon poacher, though he can be prosecuted if caught in the act of poaching, has the fish safely in his possession and away from the scene of the crime, they are his to dispose of in any way he wishes. To insist by legislation on the licensing of fish dealers would effectively block the poacher's financial motive.

Equally obviously the recommendations of the Hunter Committee that all fishing for salmonids at sea should cease is common sense. Currently whilst much is being done within the European Community to prevent wide-scale deep sea netting the case of the Faroese remains a particularly difficult one. Recent estimates of the annual open sea 'interceptary catch' as it is called shows that the Faroese take has increased five-fold over the past two years and is now estimated at around 1,000 tonnes per annum. Talks between the Faroe Islands and the EEC to attempt to limit this vast catch have proved abortive. In a community whose whole economy depends largely on fishing the Faroese unwillingness to check this golden harvest is perhaps understandable. It is only to be hoped that by closing the market for at least a proportion of the salmon, perhaps in return for providing a market for other species, this very difficult problem might be solved.

Perhaps, most importantly of all, there should be a better understanding by the general public of all the factors involved. It needs to be made clear that the great majority of salmon fishermen are not millionaires, but ordinary enthusiasts who enjoy their sport at weekends and on long summer evenings. And that the salmon provides a hard earned living for estuary netsmen in many districts. These two sides need to accept their differences and combine forces to help the salmon.

The salmon, after all, needs all the help it can get. So, at the risk of proselytising, let me recommend the work of the Salmon and Trout Association and of the Atlantic Salmon Trust.

Trawlermen repairing their net with the Faroes in the background. The Faroese catch of salmon has increased five-fold in the last two years, yet although they harvest a lucrative crop the Faroese have no salmon rivers and therefore no means of replenishing salmon stocks.

EPILOGUE

Fisherman's Prayer

God grant that I may live to fish
Until my dying day.
And when it comes to my last cast
I then most humbly pray,
When in the Lord's safe landing net
I'm peacefully asleep,
That in His mercy I be judged
As big enough to keep.